Unglued, Tattooed & Renewed

by Sara Trollinger

with

Mike Yorkey

Unglued, Tattooed & Renewed
by Sara Trollinger with Mike Yorkey

FIRST EDITION
ISBN 0-9742251-1-8
Cover and back photos: Courtesy of House of Hope
Cover and interior design: Ron Kadrmas, Colorado Springs, Colorado

To contact House of Hope:
House of Hope
P.O. Box 560503
Orlando, FL 32856
(407) 843-8686
e-mail: houseofhopesara@aol.com
Web site: www.nationalhouseofhope.org

Printed in the United States of America by Plus Communications, St. Louis, Missouri.

Dedication and Acknowledgements

This book is lovingly dedicated to the precious past and present residents of House of Hope. You are the greatest! Thank you for sharing your heart in an effort to touch other teens. Your testimonies are going to be the turning point in changing many lives.

I would like to extend my deepest gratitude to Julie Joyner for proofreading *Unglued, Tattooed & Renewed*, and to Daphne Carlisle and Laura Montgomery for their contribution in taking care of all the details.

I also want to thank Mike Yorkey for assisting me in the writing of this book. We teamed up to write *Unglued & Tattooed*, and he has helped me capture the hearts of hurting teens.

Table of Contents

foreword

by monica seles

I have visited the boys and girls at House of Hope on several occasions, and it's the coolest ministry I've ever seen. I was introduced to House of Hope by my good friends, Mark and Betsy McCormack, who have taken a vital interest in this outreach to troubled teens.

When the new Orlando campus was dedicated a few years back, I played a tennis exhibition with Betsy on the two courts donated by the McCormacks. Several hundred people watched us hit a few balls before the rains came down, but we had a great time. I pitched in by donating the funds to purchase the grandstands.

It's hard to put my finger on why House of Hope is so special, but it has to be the people. Sara Trollinger, who started the ministry, has become a warm, personal friend. Sara was a source of encouragement to me during some dark times, and from what I've seen, she is doing a remarkable job with those kids. In all my travels, I haven't seen a ministry that is more effective in restoring broken families. There is so much love there, and I am always blessed every time I visit.

But it's the young people themselves that blow me away. I can remember the times I've stopped by the House of Hope café and listened to the teenagers share their stories—stories that broke my heart because of all the abuse. No one should have to endure what these kids were put through.

I still check in from time to time with Sara and the kids. I don't get to visit as often as I would like because I live in Sarasota on Florida's West Coast, but Betsy keeps me posted. I've done a TV spot for the ministry, and several years ago, when I won the Family Circle Cup in Charleston, South Carolina, I designated House of Hope as my special charity. I also sent Sara a Yonex racket that I played with at the 1995 U.S. Open—my comeback year when I made it to the finals and barely lost. Sara says that my racket is a treasured gift.

I salute the work of House of Hope and tip my hat to the young people and parents working hard to make major changes in their lives. As I know from the tennis world, it's not easy to come back when you're down, but these kids are winners in my book.

a message

from sara trollinger

founder and president of House of Hope

Maybe your mother, a friend, or someone you know gave you this book. Perhaps you do not want to read it. You don't think any book can give you the answers you need. The truth is . . . *Unglued, Tattooed & Renewed* is the only book I know where teens speak to teens about different things they have experienced. Teens who have been unglued and tattooed will tell you how they have been renewed. As you read these real-life stories, I'm confident that you'll be able to identify with many of them.

Teenagers today are searching and crying out for the "real thing." They know the difference between genuine and plastic. They know who are the real people and who are the flimsy reproductions. What you're about to read are real stories by real teens with real answers. This book will show you how some teens took the responsibility, after a lot of hurt, to make the right choices that helped heal them and overcome their hurts. If you feel like giving up or know a teen that feels that way, I have good news for you. It doesn't have to happen!

If you are a teen facing challenges with drugs, alcohol, sex, eating disorders, body mutilation, pornography, peer pressure, and out-of-touch parents, you will be amazed at the answers you will find on these pages. If you are a parent reading this book, you'll gain great insight into the tender hearts of teens. You'll look at teenagers through a different lens when you're finished reading.

Every story told here is true. We have changed a few names in this book by request, but the things that have happened to them are real events involving real people. These teens—and several alumni that we've included—have gone through trials and temptations, but they found solutions. They want to share their stories of life-threatening problems so that your life can be spared and turned around.

Feeling down in the dumps? Hassled by parents? Looking for a dose of encouragement? If so, you've come to the right place. Fasten your seatbelts and hold on for a life-changing ride!

From my heart,

Sara

P.S. In this book, some of the teens refer to "Pastor Frank," who is Frank Reynoso, the resident pastor of House of Hope. Frank, raised in New York City, was a gang member who lived life on the edge until he came to know Christ. His background and his ability to relate to young people is what makes Frank so approachable.

making a big u-turn

by matt, sixteen

I decided very early that when my sixteenth birthday rolled around, it would be a blowout—one that I would never forget. My special evening started out fairly boring, however.

My parents made me go to the Wednesday night youth group meeting, so I complied, but only to get them off my back. Before I left the house, I told them that after youth group I was going to the movies with some friends, knowing full well that I had already made plans to drink at a friend's house with some buddies. You only turn sixteen once, right?

One of my friends knew a store where they didn't care if they sold alcohol to underage kids, so he bought quarts of Natural Ice beer and Mike's Hard Lemonade, spiked with alcohol. He bought enough to get the four of us drunk fairly quickly, including this girl we knew. I'll call her Lisa.

Lisa had driven her brand-new Ford Focus to my friend's house. After we got drunk, I asked her if I could grab a CD from her car. She gave me her keys, which turned out to be a big mistake for her.

I unlocked the car and looked for the CD. Couldn't find it. Then I had a bright idea: Why not take her car for a little joy ride? It was my sixteenth birthday, wasn't it?

I didn't have my license yet, but in my messed-up mind, I didn't care. I wanted to have some fun and see what that Ford Focus could do. I started driving like a madman through the residential streets. Lisa and my friends must have heard me burning rubber, because they came out in time to watch me fly by them at 85 mph. I was screaming!

Just one problem. The curve at the end of their street was really a cul-de-sac. I slammed on the brakes, but I ran out of pavement and plowed into some bushes between two houses, taking out a mailbox along the way. Suddenly, Lisa's new Ford Focus wasn't so new, and my joy ride wasn't so fun anymore.

Some neighbors rushed out to see what happened. All I knew was that I had to get out of there as quickly as possible! I jerked the Ford Focus into reverse, took out another mailbox, and peeled out of that cul-de-sac in a cloud of smoking rubber.

Things were happening quick. I sped back to my friend's house, where I wasn't very successful in trying to explain to Lisa why I wrecked her car. We all agreed that we had to get out of there before the cops came.

The four of us jumped into her car, and Lisa took the wheel. We were trying to find a way out of the neighborhood when a cop passed by. He flipped a

U-turn and then followed us for a few seconds before sounding his siren. Lisa didn't try to speed away, but she didn't pull over either. Meanwhile, we were tossing empty quart bottles of Natural Ice and Mike's Hard Lemonade out the windows in an attempt not to get busted. One bottle landed on the hood of the police cruiser, which infuriated the cop. I was too drunk to realize the seriousness of the moment.

When Lisa finally pulled over, we were in trouble. I was handcuffed and arrested, then taken to juvenile hall. The authorities sent me to a secular twelve-step program in another state, but I wasn't serious, which landed me in House of Hope. At first I wasn't into that religious stuff, but then I really heard God's message of salvation and accepted Christ. I started turning my life around in a hurry.

I had another court appearance coming up—a scary one. I was facing two years in an adult penitentiary after being charged with leaving the scene of an accident, driving without a license, assaulting an officer (for throwing that empty beer bottle out the window), and reckless driving.

I fasted and prayed for two days, asking God to give me mercy, and He did. The judge took away my driver's license until I turned seventeen, sentenced me to one year of probation, and ordered me to finish my program with House of Hope.

Just in case you are going through a problem with alcohol or drugs, please take my story and what I am saying seriously. The world wants you to believe that drinking is not a big deal, but it is. It almost cost me my life, and soon it could cost you yours because your next day is not promised.

The lesson I learned is that no matter how much you mess up and do stupid things, God doesn't give up on you. He is always going to be there for you, although sometimes you have to learn the hard way.

Like Jonah 3:10 says, those who turn from their evil ways will find God to be merciful. I know that I didn't deserve mercy, but because of His grace, He granted it to me anyway.

Maybe your addiction is not alcohol. It could be drugs, pornography, eating, or smoking, etc. God wants to set you free just like He did me. Would you pray a sincere prayer from your heart and turn your problems over to God? He will be there for you, too. And by the way, it's very important to find someone you can be accountable to—someone who really cares for you.

When God saw what they did and how they turned from their evil ways, he had compassion and did not bring upon them the destruction he had threatened.

—Jonah 3:10, NIV

the sleepover that changed my life

rachel, sixteen

My mom was seventeen and unmarried when she became pregnant with me. Her boyfriend did not want the responsibility of having children, so he pressured my mother to have an abortion. Mom had already been to the abortion table twice, and she didn't want to go back a third time.

I guess my father really couldn't handle the pressure because one day in his apartment, he took a gun and shot himself to death.

My mother was staggered by the suicide, which is why she may have given birth to me prematurely. I arrived seven weeks early, weighing about three pounds. My head fit in the palm of my mother's hand.

My mom decided to raise me at this point, although she didn't have any means to support us. She couldn't afford a place to live, so we lived with one of her friends. Mom struggled for years, so much so that she delivered me to the Miami Baptist Children's Home, where I would be placed for adoption. After a year in foster care, a young pastor and his wife adopted me, and they were good to me.

I was their first child, and I was happy to have real parents. As I grew older, I asked Mom and Dad if I could have a little sister. One day when I was eight years old, they took me to a restaurant and told me the good news: they were adopting a young girl. I jumped up and down in my chair because I was so excited.

I wasn't a bad child growing up. I think everyone assumed that I was a Christian because my dad was an associate pastor, but I never accepted Christ in my younger years. I acted like a Christian, though, just like any good person would.

Everything was fine until November 23, 2001, a date that I will never forget. I was fourteen, and my parents had gone to a church conference. They had my sister stay at Grandma's house, and they let me stay with Melanie, one of my friends at the Christian school I was attending.

After her parents had gone to bed, Melanie and I talked in her bedroom. She had an older brother named Matt, who was seventeen. I thought he was cute, so I told Melanie that. She thought it was funny, and she teased me about it, which is what fourteen-year-old girls do.

She got up and walked across the hall into Matt's bedroom, where he was watching TV. She said something to him, and when she came back, she told me I should go say hello to her brother. I protested, but she gently pushed me out the door.

Then she locked me out. I banged on the door, but she would not let me back in.

"Can I help you?" Matt asked, standing in his doorway.

"Your sister won't let me in," I said.

"Why don't you come watch some TV with me?" he said, flashing a smile.

It turned out that Matt wanted to do a lot more than watch TV. He shut the door and locked it, and before I knew it, he was forcing himself on me. He raped me and stole my virginity in a matter of minutes. Up until then, I had never done so much as go out with a boy, let alone kiss one. Now I had been raped.

I got up and left. Melanie had unlocked her room. When she asked how I was, I pretended everything was fine. I didn't tell her what happened. I couldn't. I kept my mouth shut, so she had no idea.

I didn't tell anyone what Matt had done. I felt very guilty. It must have been my fault, something I said. I felt so dirty after the experience that for the next six months, I would take six showers a day in a vain attempt to rid myself of how dirty I felt.

I remember a cute guy at my school taking an interest in me, but all he had to do was touch me on the shoulder, and I would freak out. I couldn't pay attention in class. I couldn't focus on what my teachers were saying, and I walked around like I was in a fog when I was with Jake, my new boyfriend.

One morning when I was taking a shower, I was shaving my legs when I gave myself a huge cut. As I watched the blood dribble down my leg, I noticed that it didn't hurt. Actually, cutting myself felt like a release of the tension that had been building up within me.

I liked that feeling, so I began cutting myself more and more. I usually used a steak knife or a razor blade. I gouged my arms and my rib cage in an attempt to release the emotional pain that had built up inside me. If I didn't cut myself at night, I couldn't face the next day.

The cuts and jabs left scars on my arms and torso, so I covered up by wearing sweatshirts everywhere I went. That wasn't easy in hot and humid Florida, but it shows how desperate I was to hide what I was doing.

I kept cutting and cutting myself, and I would bleed a lot. One time I took nail clippers and used it to rip out chunks of flesh from my wrists. I lost a lot of blood doing that. I hid an old towel in my bedroom closet and used that to wipe up the blood. I would wash the towel whenever my parents were gone for a while.

My parents never suspected anything because I was always a good kid. Then my grandpa died, and I went to the funeral with Jake. After the memorial service, we went to my grandma's house, where my boyfriend and I slipped away to the basement. The sadness of losing my grandfather hit me so hard. I started crying, and Jake held me close, and before we knew it, he lost his virginity to me. I didn't want to do it, but I thought if we didn't have sex, then he wouldn't love me anymore.

After that happened, we were physical almost every time we saw each other. Sex became something that was expected by him. After months of sexual activity, Jake broke up with me before Christmas. That tore me up. I thought that if I had sex with him and he still didn't want me, what was I worth then? I got even more depressed, so I kept cutting myself with a vengeance.

One time Mom wanted to see a new shirt that I was wearing, so I had to take off my sweatshirt in front of Mom.

"What's that?" she asked, pointing at my arms.

"Oh, somebody must have scratched me with her fingernails," I said, as I quickly put my sweatshirt back on.

"No, I want to see your arms," Mom said.

I refused to take off my sweatshirt. Dad entered the fray, and he demanded that I remove the sweatshirt. When I finally complied, he saw what I had done to my arms. He began crying and soon got me into some counseling, but that didn't help at all.

When I told my father that I wasn't getting any help, he and Mom put me in a crisis unit at a nearby hospital for two weeks. I came home and began acting weird: I ran away, downed a bottle of prescription pills and half a bottle of prescription painkillers (it's God's grace that I survived), and wondered if I should kill myself with a knife or razor—the ultimate release.

My parents drove me back to the crisis unit at the hospital, where I was diagnosed with post-traumatic stress disorder, severe depression, and panic disorder. My parents then started looking into long-term programs because they said they couldn't keep me safe. That's when they found House of Hope.

When I arrived, I was extremely mad. I was mad

at my parents for making me come here. I'll never forget walking into the main office and seeing this huge painting of Jesus. I thought He was staring at me and judging me, just like other Christians I had known. As far as I was concerned, Christians were nothing but a bunch of hypocrites. They had made my life miserable at my old school. They said I was ugly, but when I got a modeling job, they said I wasn't pretty enough. They called me "Roach" because my nickname is "Rache."

When I moved into my residential home at House of Hope, I didn't talk to anyone. Whenever anyone tried to start a conversation, I blew them off. I didn't want anything to do with anybody.

Something intrigued me during our chapel services, however. I saw kids my age fall on their knees in worship. What were they doing? I grew up in the church, and I had never seen that before. So I started talking a little bit to some people. Certain girls really reached out to me. They surrounded me with love. They told me I was beautiful and that they loved me and that God loved me.

I tried to brush them off, though. "You don't know what you're talking about," I said. "You don't know what I've done in my life."

They kept loving me. I didn't realize it, but God was molding my heart. He was rearranging a lot of furniture. One night at chapel, there were a bunch of people singing and praising God, and the Lord just broke me. He started showing me all the things in my life that He could touch, like my open wounds. I didn't want to show the others any emotion, but the dam burst. I just started sobbing so hard in my seat, and then I felt what I had never felt before—an incredible feeling of someone wrapping His arms around me. Jesus was bringing me close to Him, and then several teens wrapped their arms around me and told me how much they loved me.

Ashley offered to walk up to the altar with me, where I kneeled and accepted Christ into my heart. Pastor Frank, our resident pastor who leads our chapel services, led me in prayer, and something inside me changed to peace and joy.

This happened on April 9, the day before my birthday. In the future, I will be having a two-day birthday party—the anniversary when I got saved, and the anniversary when I was born.

I feel beautiful now. I know I don't feel gross any-more. I'm beautiful because Jesus Christ has made me so.

I know that there are a lot of girls and guys who are cutting themselves today looking for a release from their hurts. If you can identify with anything I've gone through—adoption, rejection, rape, sex, cutting, or feeling ashamed and ugly—please don't give up. Cry out to Jesus, and He'll be there for you. He will definitely change your life, just like He changed mine.

Therefore, if anyone is in Christ, he is a new creation; the old has gone, the new has come!

—2 Corinthians 5:17, NIV

the power of friends

brian, sixteen

I was doing fine until I hit fifth grade and met Kevin. After we became friends, he introduced me to his buddies. We looked out for each other, especially when we started stealing stuff from stores.

One of the guys would say, "Hey, let's do a beer run," so we'd walk over to the Cumberland Farms mini mart store and case the place. I would walk to the back where they kept the beer behind the refrigerated glass doors. Our beer of choice was Red Dog, so when the clerk was busy ringing up a customer, I would grab two quarts, act like I was looking for the bathroom, and then sprint out of the back door. I did most of the stealing.

I was usually gone before the stupid clerk knew what was happening, but one time a lady chased us in her van. She found my friends, but they told her that they didn't know where I went. When the coast was clear, we shared the beer, which got us drunk.

Growing up in the Miami area, it seemed as

though I was always getting in trouble. By the time I reached seventh grade, I was kicked out of school. My parents signed me up for some type of Christian boarding program where I came home on the weekends. I know that Mom and Dad had their hands full trying to raise my two brothers and two sisters and at the same time dealing with my problems.

I got suspended from school twenty times, constantly stole candy, sodas, and other food items, and constantly got arrested. The local cops and shop owners came to know me well because they knew I couldn't go into a store without stealing something.

My parents knew they had to do something, so Mom moved the family to Orlando so that I would no longer hang out with my old friends. Dad commuted to his accounting job in Miami and would stay down there during the week, coming home on weekends.

It wasn't long before I started making new friends—friends who became so important that I basically stopped going to school. I didn't like hanging around home because I constantly got into fights with Jenny, my sister who was six years older.

Because Dad was gone all the time, I felt as though I should be the man of the house. Jenny would get on the phone and make these long-distance calls to her old friends back in Miami, and I didn't like her running up the phone bill. So I would give her a smack to get off the phone, but she didn't appreciate my efforts to save the family money. Several times she called the cops, and I was given a domestic violence charge.

I got back at her. Every once in a while, I would steal Jenny's car, and half the time she didn't know about it. I also started stealing *from* cars—stereos, money, whatever I could find in there. I did it to get some money to buy weed.

Meanwhile, the Orlando cops were learning my name, and my brushes with the law earned me a trip to a court-ordered school, but I kept getting into more trouble. I got arrested so many times that I knew how to put my hands in the correct position—behind my back, hands together, fingers pointing downward—to make it easier for the cop to slap the 'cuffs on me.

The last time I got arrested, I knew this judge was going to be tough. I expected the worst—to be sent to a lockdown facility for eight to sixteen months. This judge had heard about House of Hope, though, and this is where I landed.

House of Hope is where I heard the Gospel for the first time and where I learned how important it is to surround yourself with good friends. You see, I always got in trouble because the people I used to hang out with were up to no good. Since they were up to no good, I was up to no good.

I can see now why one of the rules at House of Hope is that you can't see old friends from your past. I used to break it, but now I see the importance of having friends who can have a positive influence on me.

This I do know: The more I make good friends, the less bad things happen to me.

A righteous man is cautious in friendship, but the way of the wicked leads them astray.

—*Proverbs 12:26, NIV*

when hope won out

hope, seventeen

I made the decision rather matter-of-factly: I was going to end my life. At seventeen, I was a dropout with a lot of issues and self-image problems. My problems started when I was just seven years old. I was walking home from school one afternoon when a man in a car pulled up beside me.

The man jumped out of the car asked me, "Will you help me find my puppy?"

"What did you say, Mister?"

I never received an answer. The man grabbed me and threw me in the car. He held me down in the front seat while he drove us to a secluded area. Then he proceeded to brutalize me for nearly two hours. He raped me at least twice, and then he inserted a hairbrush into me. I screamed for my mother, but no one came to save me.

For the next few years, I would wake up in the middle of the night crying because of an intense pain between my legs. Mom and the doctors could never figure out why until I told Mom what had happened. She believed me, but she had her own problems to contend with—like my father.

By the time I entered middle school, Dad was destroying himself with drugs and alcohol. One night, he got drunk and exposed himself to me. Then he urinated on me. I had tried to forget the horrible rape, but following that terrible incident, I felt ugly, worthless—like I had been deflowered. Then my father abandoned Mom and me.

Things were going bad in high school. I was hearing voices a lot, and I thought I was going crazy. It would be better to end it all, I decided, so I found a small bottle of ibuprofen and washed down between fifty and one hundred pills. After I swallowed all those capsules, I started crying uncontrollably. I was home at the time, and when my mother asked me why, I told her what I had done.

Mom immediately called Poison Control, where a counselor warned that I could go into a coma and convulsions at any moment. Paramedics rushed to our home, but I was so hostile that they had to tie my arms to the stretcher while they transferred me to the emergency room. The restraints were cinched tighter when ER doctors began pumping my stomach to rid myself of the ibuprofen overdose. What an awful experience!

Once I recovered, I was shipped to a juvenile mental hospital. I was locked down with other adolescents who were schizophrenic—boys and girls restrained with straightjackets and sedated half the time with calming drugs. Most of them were on so much medication that if you asked them what color the ceiling was, they couldn't tell you.

I thought I was going psycho, too. I was assigned to a room where everything was bolted down to the floor—the bed, a single chair, and a table. I was not allowed to have any pencils, pens, glass containers, earrings, or jewelry—nothing. High up in one corner was a camera, so I was watched twenty-four hours a day. Even when I used the toilet in my room, I was watched. That was spooky.

I was let out during the day to the "community room," where I ate my meals and watched TV with the rest of the "residents." We were served what I call prison food, which was wheeled out in these huge heating trays. I could tell the kitchen staff didn't care about us because our trays were heated on one side, so I usually ended up with Jell-O soup and some type of cold, gross-looking chicken. I could never identify the orange, green, or red vegetables on my plate, and the lumpy potatoes were awful. They gave us little cups filled with a concentrated drink that was so disgusting that I preferred to drink from the water fountain.

And our days! All of the kids sat on lumpy couches and wooden chairs like bumps on a log, staring at a TV tuned to the Cartoon Channel from morning until night. Watching cartoons all day long may sound like fun, but it got pretty old!

Finally, after a week, my mom was able to get me out of there. The judge placed me into a residential program at House of Hope. My sister had gone here a few years before, so we knew that people like me received help.

What I've learned since being at House of Hope is

that by believing in God, I am going somewhere and I am somebody. God really cares who I am. I have also learned that God doesn't owe us any favors. We are to take each day as it comes and try to make the most of it for His glory.

My hurting past is no fault of my own, but either way, I was going down the world's path until I learned there was a better route by being led by Jesus Christ. I'm going to follow His path because Jesus has given me back my self-respect and has promised to restore what was brutally taken from me—my childhood. God will be as big in your life as you will allow Him to be.

There is a special prayer I prayed at House of Hope, and it sums up my story. Maybe you have had some hurts like me. You can pray the prayer that I prayed:

Dear God,

My life has been a big mess. I know that I wouldn't be alive, but You protected me. Thank you for always being there, even in the worst times. Thank you Jesus that You have healed the little child in me and that You have given me my childhood back. Now I can laugh again.

In Your Precious name. Amen.

Great is the Lord and most worthy of praise; his greatness no one can fathom.

—Psalms 145:3, NIV

working both sides of the street

tim, seventeen

At the end of sixth grade, my mom was diagnosed with breast cancer. That hit me pretty hard. She went through chemotherapy and radiation for several months, leaving home every Friday for chemo and sometimes staying overnight. The side effects were pretty bad.

I had to grow up fast. My father dealt with the news by staying away from home as much as possible and going to church every time the doors were open. He owned an engineering company, so he hung out there. I guess that was his form of escape, but he should have visited Mom in the hospital. If I wanted to go, I had to walk there or get my grandparents to drive me.

When Mom was home, she was on all kinds of drugs. She would trip out on morphine to the point where she didn't know who she was or where she was. I had two younger sisters, and it was all we could do to cope.

I don't know why Dad couldn't handle it. He had

it in his mind that Mom did some great sin against God, so the cancer was His way of punishing her for what she had done. Mom knew she had been abandoned. As soon as she was off chemo, she filed for divorce.

Dad has always tried to control her life. If Mom wanted to go shopping at Wal-Mart, she had to ask permission and tell him where she was going. She wasn't allowed to have any girlfriends. Dad made her stop working when I was born, but she didn't want to do that. If she had stayed at the big CPA firm where she worked, she could have become a managing partner. Mom was a talented accountant who graduated from Wake Forest and Stetson University.

Mom had tried to get them to go to counseling before, but he said they didn't need counseling and God would heal the relationship. Mom got tired of waiting for God to fix things. The divorce was granted when I was in the middle of seventh grade.

Dad said he had always wanted to become a missionary, but after the divorce, he was mad not because she was gone, but because he had lost stature in the eyes of the church. They split custody of the three children right down the middle. Mom moved into a home two doors away; Dad kept the same house. He had built it, and it was his pride and joy. They agreed that we would live with Mom for the first semester of school and with Dad during the second semester. The first part of summer, we lived with Mom, and the second part of summer was with Dad. Every other weekend, we switched homes.

Living in two homes on the same street was convenient. We never had any problems at Mom's house, but if things got too heated at Dad's, we could run down to her house. The divorce didn't bother me at all. I was happy to see it happen to Dad because I didn't like him. I hated what he put Mom through. He'd say things like, "What sin have you done to make God punish you?" He was against the drugs. He couldn't understand that the drugs were keeping her alive. He thought she should pray about her cancer and accept the will of God.

I still played football and basketball throughout middle school. But my attitude for working hard went way down when I was introduced to drugs and alcohol. By my freshman year, I was only playing basketball. This was also the year that Mom met a guy named Joe. Dad had nothing but negative things to say about that. When he found out that Mom slept with Joe, he called her a whore. I tried to defend Mom, but Dad was insistent that she was engaging in "impure things" and setting a horrible example for us. He was still down on them when they got married.

Dad didn't know that I was involved in sexual activity, too. I had told myself that I would wait until high school, so I waited one week into my freshman year. I was smoking pot and drinking quarts of Olde English beer because it was cheap. The manager of a Quik Stop convenience store would sell it to us, but only when no one else was in the store. Of course, he also padded the bill when he sold to minors. A six-pack cost $5; quarts went for $1.50. I don't think my parents suspected anything because I was still playing basketball and pulling a 3.5 grade point average.

The summer before tenth grade was horrible. Mom would leave the house at 7:30 to work at a CPA firm. My friends would come over and smoke weed in the backyard; then we'd go to clubs at night. To finance my new lifestyle, I sold drugs or acted as a middleman. Whenever I sold to kids, I would gyp them, giving them half the drugs they paid for.

I liked selling beans, or little pills, to Daddy's little girl. They were "dirty" because they were laced with heroin. I sold beans for $15-$20 a pill; they cost me between $5 and $8. I never kept the drugs on me. I would get their money and go to my friend's house and buy for them. I made at least $100 each trip.

Most of the girls wanted ecstasy, though. Ecstasy made them feel good, made them feel beautiful. Their rich dads had given them all this money for clothes, but they would use it to buy pills and get high so that they could have sex with people they did not want to have sex with, but that's what ecstasy does to you.

My parents never wondered how I could buy so many CDs, PlayStation games, and new clothes. I worked at McDonalds to fool them, but I soon found out that it was an easy place to sell from. I made sure I worked the back window, and people I knew would order a Big Mac meal at the drive-thru, but when they pulled up, I knew they wanted something more than a few extra ketchup packets. It was amusing how easy it was, selling drugs at McDonalds. It did wonders for my popularity.

I stopped caring about school because I didn't think I needed it. I was making an easy $500 a week selling drugs. I began getting straight Fs. My parents tried to change me, but they were powerless.

One weekend, I knew Dad would be gone until Monday night, so I threw a little party at the house.

We turned Dad's house into party central. The entire senior class was there and most of my high school; around 700 kids showed up. We had a few kegs in the garage, and all kinds of drugs. People were injecting cocaine or sniffing crack off my dad's kitchen counters.

When it was over, the white tile had turned black, and the garage floor reeked of stale beer. I had a couple of friends come over to help me clean on Sunday, but we used that as an excuse to do more drinking and smoking.

I don't know what happened, but when my father arrived home on Monday night, he found me passed out drunk on his couch. I eventually got sent to Teen Challenge boot camp in Bonifay, Florida. I was mad because it was a Christian boot camp. You don't live. You survive. They try to break you. You don't see your parents or your family. Teen Challenge was hell for me, but I did good in it.

Then my parents suddenly pulled me from Teen Challenge and brought me to House of Hope. But I had already rededicated my life to Christ at Teen Challenge. I knew I had to stop my self-destructive behavior. It was only by the grace of God that I never got caught. The cops had caught on to me, and they were getting close to arresting me. They had raided my friend's house, and his two older brothers were sent to prison. That shook me because I knew I was next.

I had a hard time rededicating my life to Christ, though. Whenever I looked at my father, I said to myself, *If God is supposed to be like a father to me, would He be like that guy?* I never wanted to grow up like my father. But as I learned more about who God was, I came to realize that God is the father

I'm *supposed* to have—a father who loves me unconditionally, who looks out for my well-being, and who wants to be my friend. He can be stern but fair.

I would characterize my walk with Christ as growing. I'm a work in progress. I know I am not a super Christian, but it's more of a personal thing now. I read my Bible and pray. I'm very obedient now. I don't get in trouble. I know right from wrong. I have a sober mind, and I'm really pleased to say that my relationship with Mom and Dad is better than it was. I can even stand to be in the same house with them.

That is definitely what I would call a miracle. Just in case you are having some problems at home like I did, you, too, can give God a chance. He's the only one who can change your life and give you hope for the future.

For by the grace given me I say to every one of you: Do not think of yourself more highly than you ought, but rather think of yourself with sober judgment, in accordance with the measure of faith God has given you.

—Romans 12:3, NIV

when life was a big lie

angela, seventeen

Like many young people who end up at House of Hope, I grew up in an abusive home environment. My dad hit me with belts and choked me for arguing with my little brother, Andrew. Mom didn't lift a finger to help me. That's because Dad pushed and hit her when he didn't like something she did or said.

You could say that my mom's side of the family was mentally unstable. I had three uncles commit suicide: one set himself on fire, another shot himself in the head, and the third walked in front of a semi. My grandparents were just as wacko. One time, a black family moved into the neighborhood, but they hated blacks, so my grandparents set the house on fire. That landed my grandmother into a mental institution for a while. Another time, I was driving in the car with my grandfather when he saw someone pedaling a bike. He didn't like cyclists hogging the road, so he tapped him with his car. The boy fell and hit the pavement, getting all scraped up. Grandfather thought it was the most hilarious thing he ever saw.

He also thought it was funny to lock my grandmother in her bedroom for days at a time. The only time he allowed the door to open was when he gave her food. Another time, my grandparents were looking after my great-uncle Joe, who had multiple sclerosis. He used a morphine drip to deal with the pain, but my grandparents stole the morphine and injected it into themselves. Everyone thought that was funny.

This all seemed normal to me growing up. I didn't think anything of it. Though I never received any formal lessons, I learned how to lie and manipulate people. I was also a brat. I remember one time when I got new shoes from my grandparents. I was in the car with my dad, and he got mad at me for something, so he threatened to throw my new shoes out the window. "I don't care," I replied. "Grammy will buy me a new pair." So Dad threw them out. I remember my grandmother being really upset at my father for doing this, but I did get another pair. Another time, I found some needles and used them to make little pinprick holes in my waterbed. Then I blamed my little brother.

"Mom, Mom, look what Andrew did!" I enjoyed watching Andrew get spanked.

My whole life was a big lie. When I got older, I lied about where I was going, who I would be with, and what I would do. I cheated at school. Before class, I would get other people's homework and copy it. When we took tests, I peaked at the answers on my neighbor's test when the teacher wasn't looking.

My cheating wasn't enough to keep me from failing, however. I flunked sixth, seventh, and eighth grades, but each June, the school administration said if I would go to summer school, then they would pass me. I think this is what they call "social promotion."

The biggest cheating going on, however, was watching Mom cheat on my dad when I was in middle school. She went out almost every evening while Dad stayed home with Andrew and me. Whenever I asked where Mom was, Dad said she was out with her friends. It wasn't long before Dad moved out, and Mom's boyfriend moved in—one week after the breakup. As soon as the divorce was final, Mom married Bill, and he became my new stepdad.

That made me very angry. I didn't understand who I was or who my parents were. I screamed at Bill, telling him he wasn't my real dad, and I didn't want him in my house. I threatened to make up stories that he was abusing me and would call the cops on him. Mom threw up her hands and shuttled me back and forth from Dad's house. Whenever things got hot in one household, I would run back to the other house.

Everyone at school hated me. They called me a slut because I was sleeping around with guys, which was true. I started sleeping around with high school guys when I was in eighth grade. One right after another; I probably slept with fifteen guys. Sometimes I had sex on the first date, if I liked the guy. When I was in ninth grade, I had a boyfriend who was nineteen years old who had his own place.

It was easy to stay with him, and we were together for about six months. How I never got pregnant is a miracle.

I got wilder. I had started smoking more weed, doing some cocaine, and trying ecstasy once or twice. I hated my life in ninth grade, and I felt suicidal. I started saying things like, "I'm going to kill myself because I hate myself" when I was around Mom. She responded by sending me to Lifestreams, a treatment center for suicidal teens.

I actually enjoyed Lifestreams because I was away from Mom. I still felt suicidal. After I got released, I told one of the girls at my private school that I was planning to kill myself. She ratted on me with the principal, and they kicked me out.

I moved in with Dad, who was sympathetic because he had found God. "Things will be okay," he said soothingly. "It's like a new start." We decided that I would homeschool and get some counseling.

Things went well for a couple of months until I got involved with a seventeen-year-old guy that I met online. I was fourteen when we agreed to meet each other at the mall. This relationship was different because I was sexually experienced, and he wasn't. I took control, and within a month, he lost his virginity with me. We were together for about eight months.

Meanwhile, Dad was trying to get me to go to church, but I didn't want to go. Our relationship got rocky, but Mom wouldn't take me back for anything. My counselor suggested to my dad that he send me to House of Hope. When I heard about that news,

I flipped out. I was in denial.

"I'm not going to no House of Hope," I said.

"Angie, you need to go," replied my father. "You need some help, girl."

That was April 2000. When I arrived, I met Tony. He talked to me about God, but I was mean to him. He was just trying to be nice, but I found the whole thing weird. I never listened to what the speakers were saying in chapel. After a while, though, my heart softened some to Christ, but I didn't give my heart to Him. It was more of a front. I thought it was a way to graduate from House of Hope.

I moved on up in the program and started "home phase," which meant I could live at home for longer and longer periods. I still hated my life. I was so lost. I started cutting myself by taking a safety pin and sticking it into the side of my leg. I did it for attention. Meanwhile, I fought depression and fought with my parents continually. Dad decided I needed to return to House of Hope again.

It was during my *second* stay that I found God and thought I had turned things around when I graduated in December 2001 from House of Hope. I was wrong again. I was keeping in touch with Miss Rosie, my old houseparent. "I need to come back," I told her. "And I really need prayer." So I returned to House of Hope a *third* time, even though it was a humbling experience to admit that I still needed help. I knew I needed it, though.

One time, I was meeting with one of the volunteer prayer women, Miss Darlene, in the Lighthouse, a building we have on campus that looks just like a lighthouse. She prayed for me that day, and something happened to break the bonds that Satan had wrapped around me. I felt God's forgiveness in a way I never felt before. I confessed everything to her.

It's been an amazing ride: it's like I have nothing to hide. I feel free. I was so used to living a lie, but now I know who I am. I don't have to live a lie. I can trust in the Lord with all my heart, lean not on my own understanding, but in all my ways acknowledge Him, knowing that He will make my paths straight.

My relationship with God is awesome! My advice to people my age is don't run from your problems and don't live a lie. You're not fooling God, who knows everything. Instead, He wants you to come to Him so that He can help you. You can get up off the floor if you fall. I've tripped way too many times, but each time, God helped me get back up.

I'm hoping to go to college so that I can become a counselor and a massage therapist. I would like to counsel others while I work on their muscles. That sounds neat to me. I could counsel and massage people in mind, body, and spirit. I want to serve God and help people wipe their past away.

Please don't let your life be a big lie like mine was before I met Jesus.

Truthful lips endure forever, but a lying tongue lasts only a moment.

—Proverbs 12:19, NIV

a time bomb waiting to explode

lewannah, thirty

It's hard to believe that half a lifetime ago I arrived at House of Hope. It certainly seems like I've packed several lifetimes into three decades on this earth. Like most kids who come to House of Hope, I grew up in a dysfunctional home. Mom and Dad were drug addicts, but when he became very abusive to her, she opted out of the relationship.

Mom worked three jobs while my grandmother watched my younger brother and me. My grandmother, a former Sunday school teacher, got into the witch-craft and the warlock thing, however, and her second husband sexually abused me when I was six or seven years old. Then Grandma disappeared one day when I was eight years old, and we haven't seen her since that day. We don't know if she is even alive.

I was a good kid until I was twelve—ironically the same year my mom got saved. Mom became a holy-roller type, and I wanted none of that stuff. I became very rebellious. I shaved my head, disappeared for weeks at a time, stole money from my mother, and beat up her and my younger brother. I got into the punk scene in the late 1980s and pierced myself and got tattoos long before they were cool. I had my nose pierced and pierced my ears at least thirteen times.

I shoplifted whatever I could: cheap jewelry, bras, underwear, and makeup—those sorts of things. I never did drugs, though, because my dad had been an addict. I did drink a ton of beer. I liked to drink myself to oblivion because that way I didn't have to feel anything anymore.

I was heavily into boys, as well, and lost my virginity when I was fifteen. I had no respect for anybody. I mean zero. I felt as though everyone owed me something. I acted clearly in the victim mode. I got caught stealing my mom's car because a cop recognized me. All the cops knew me in my hometown, and when I appeared in court, the judge said he was sorely tempted to lock me up until I was twenty-one years old.

I think I acted this way because I had experienced a lot of rejection. I didn't have a dad, a normal grandma, or any uncles or aunts. I was angry with my mother because after she got saved, she laid down all these stupid rules, like no listening to secular music. As I kept getting into trouble, she knew that she was outmatched. She heard about House of Hope through her church, so one day she drove me from our home in Tampa over to Orlando. She dropped me off and left. All I had was a suitcase of clothes. Back then, House of Hope was all girls—no boys.

I like to joke that we had more hard-core girls

back in my day, but when Mom dropped me off, I was scared. I knew something had to change. My house mom was Brenda, and she was made for me. I was hungry to learn and change and live a different way. She talked to me about things like forgiveness, and she planted seeds in me that she's still watering all these years later.

Even today I still call Brenda every couple of months. I know I needed her love and counsel when I got into a bad relationship with the father of my three kids. I was caught in a living hell for three years, and I started drinking heavily again because I didn't want to feel the pain. But the seeds that Brenda planted reminded me to take an honest inventory of myself. She reminded me that the Christian faith is all about perseverance.

Now I'm a single-parent mom living in Southern California. We live with my mom, who has been a wonderful help. My kids are ten, eight, and six, so I have my hands full. I'm attending college full time with the goal of earning a degree in applied sciences and computer management systems. I'm still very stubborn, and it seems that I still have to learn things the hard way.

I'm grateful for the lessons I learned at House of Hope—that God is watching out for me, that He has a plan for my life, and that I should stay close to Him. When I tell people that House of Hope should be renamed the House of Miracles, I really mean it. For fifteen years, they've always been there when I've needed help. I'll never forget the time House of Hope helped me and my mom with rent money when we were destitute.

My advice to teens is to listen to people who have experienced what you are going through. They will say that there are other ways to deal with your pain than acting out. Talk about what's bothering you. Don't hold it in. I held everything in until I was a bomb ready to explode. Accept that you are not in control. Trust in the Lord, and He will take care of you.

That's a promise He will keep for you because He has kept it for me. Don't give up hope because I made it, and you can make it too.

He who dwells in the shelter of the Most High will rest in the shadow of the Almighty. I will say of the Lord, "He is my refuge and my fortress, my God, in whom I trust." You will not fear the terror of night, nor the arrow that flies by day, nor the pestilence that stalks in the darkness, nor the plague that destroys at midday. A thousand may fall at your side, ten thousand at your right hand, but it will not come near you.

You will only observe with your eyes and see the punishment of the wicked. If you make the Most High your dwelling—even the Lord, who is my refuge—then no harm will befall you, no disaster will come near your tent.

For he will command his angels concerning you to guard you in all your ways; they will lift you up in their hands, so that you will not strike your foot against a stone.

—Psalms 91:1-2, 5-12, NIV

dealing with addictions

josh, seventeen

My story begins when my parents divorced when I was less than one year old. Mom left Dad because he sexually abused my older sister, who was fourteen at the time. It wasn't a one-time occurrence; authorities later determined that my father had taken advantage of my sister eight times. Dad was sent to prison for six years.

That made Mom and Dad both three-time losers at marriage. Unfortunately, Mom didn't find out until after the divorce that her third husband had been imprisoned for sexually abusing other children.

Mom remarried a fourth time to Steve, who became my stepdad. When my real dad got out of prison, he wanted to spend time with me and my real brothers, but his court-ordered visits had to be supervised by Mom or a well-trusted friend.

I began counseling when I was in first grade, probably because of all the family upheaval. I was an angry kid, violent with others, used to throwing chairs and displaying a bad attitude. "What are we going to do with you?" my guidance counselor asked. "What are we going to do?"

She referred to what I call a "play doctor"—someone who watches you from behind a mirror while you play with blocks and other toys. I guess they wanted to try to figure out what was going through my head. Another time the play doctor asked me to draw a picture, so I drew a picture of my dad behind bars, which was pretty powerful.

In third grade, I was funneled into an EH class, which means a class for the emotionally handicapped. I stayed in EH until fifth grade. I never had any friends except for kids in that class. That was hard for me. I wanted to make friends with other kids at school, but they segregated the EH kids from the normal kids.

When I left the EH program in middle school, I started fighting and becoming more violent. If I didn't get my way, or if some guy got on my nerves, I decked him with my fists. I was constantly suspended. This type of behavior landed me in House of Hope when I was thirteen—a seventh grader.

I stayed for thirteen months, graduated, and went back home, although I returned every Tuesday night for outpatient counseling. I was a powder keg waiting to blow, and it happened when I entered the tenth grade as I arrived in the full-blown teenage years. I met the wrong crowd and began smoking marijuana and drinking lots of alcohol.

It's not that I didn't know God. I had gotten saved back in middle school at my parents' church. But when I entered the tenth grade, I eventually lost motivation and stopped going to church on Sunday and Wednesday night youth group. My new motivation was now taking drugs and having as much sex as I could. I did these things to fill a void inside my heart—a void caused by my father's rejection of me. He showed favorites and chose to spend more time with my brothers. The only time he showed any interest in me was when he wanted to show me a new pornographic magazine or some porn site on the computer.

I became addicted to pornography and addicted to sex because I wanted to try what I saw. I would find new girls to sleep with or use the same girl multiple times. I thought that was the best thing in the world.

Then I got busted.

I was over at my girlfriend's house, and I had just set up a video camera to film what we were about to do when her parents came back early. They caught us, and boy, did I get in trouble with Mom and Steve. They began drug-testing me as well, which I failed four times.

That was the last straw. The following Saturday, my parents said I was going back to House of Hope. Now I'm a two-time guy, but did I learn? No. I continued to do drugs on weekends when I got home passes.

I was so sick of the life I was living. I asked Mr. Angel, my house staff at House of Hope, if he could pray for me, and something dramatic happened when he asked God to deliver me from drugs, alcohol, and the party scene. It happened! I lost all my desire for drugs and alcohol overnight.

I have a much stronger relationship with the Lord now. I get into worship and prayer and being a leader in the house. I have no desire to go back to my old life. I don't care if people think I'm a Christian now. I want to tell my old friends that I'm a Christian because Jesus has been faithful and has never given up on me.

To those of you reading this who've been in the same shoes as me, please learn from my mistakes. Don't try to fill that void with alcohol, sex, pornography, and drugs. You can pray the same prayer that Mr. Angel prayed with me:

Dear God, thank you for giving me authority over the strongholds in my life. Satan, I command you to go now in Jesus' name. I refuse to follow your evil ways. Jesus, I give You these areas of my life where I've tried to fill the void left by rejection from my father. Give me the strength to receive comfort from You as my heavenly Father.

In Your precious name. Amen.

Delight yourself in the Lord and he will give you the desires of your heart.

—Psalms 37:4, NIV

waking up with a knife at my throat

laura, sixteen

I was always a happy, smiley type of kid until my parents got divorced when I was seven years old. Dad stopped coming around. I had one older brother, and even though Daniel was almost four years older than I was, I had to raise him because he was so immature—he couldn't do anything. I cooked and cleaned for him, made sure he did his homework, and asked him who he was going out with.

Mom worked as a medical assistant in a doctor's office that treated cancer patients. That's kind of a downer, but she was good at it. We lived in New York City, but we moved a lot—nine times in four years, but that's because my dad wasn't paying child support and we couldn't pay the bills. We mainly lived in Queens so that we could go the same school and keep all the same friends.

When Daniel got into high school, he started hitting me because he was angry that he had nobody in his life but his little sister and his mom. He had no guys in his life, and he thought it was his fault. My dad, who was a New York City firefighter, was an alcoholic and usually drunk whenever we saw him.

When I was in middle school, I got into smoking and drugs. Daniel stopped going to school altogether. Mom was totally clueless because she was working all the time. Then she got sick with MS—multiple sclerosis—but she had to keep working so that we could keep the rent paid and food on the table. I don't know how she did it. The worst blow was when my brother wrecked our car. We had no money to fix it, so Mom walked three miles to work because she didn't have the money for the bus fare.

I took it hard and totally went downhill. In eighth and ninth grade, I drank beer and did drugs. I liked hanging out with gangs, and I was part of the crews that hung around the Crips or LK, or Latin Kings.

Mom knew things weren't good, so she took the drastic step of moving us to Florida when I was fifteen years old because we had family in Orlando. My brother stayed in New York, however, and moved in with Dad. What a mess. He started going to college, but when my father didn't pay the college bills, he had to drop out.

The first guy I met in Orlando was Johnny—twenty-one years old, married with two kids, and working in construction. I had just turned fifteen. I met him at a mall, where he said he was in the middle of a separation. He swept me off my feet. I gave him my virginity, but after that, he became very abusive to me. He used a lot of f-words as adjectives, saying that I was stupid, my mom was a whore, and he accused me of sleeping around behind his back. He told me I was only breaking up so I could have sex with other guys.

But of course, he loved me.

At least, that's what he said. This relationship lasted two months until I broke up with him for good.

I fell into a group of Venezuelan guys with nice cars. They drove cars like Porsches 911s, Honda Preludes, and Mitsubishi Eclipses. The head guy of this group was Luis—suave, beautiful, and rich. His family had a beautiful house, and he drove a beautiful car—a Spyder Eclipse with all the trim.

Luis, four years older than me at nineteen, liked to party hard. We pounded down Budweisers but we didn't do drugs. Within a month after we started dating, we were saying "I love you" to each other. We also expressed that love in a physical manner. Most of the time we used protection, but three times we didn't.

One afternoon, Mom asked, "Are you pregnant?"

"Mom, you must be out of your mind. You don't know what you're talking about," I chastised her.

Come to think of it, I was late with my period, but I couldn't imagine myself being pregnant. I shrugged off her question and continued to sneak into Mom's bathroom and take some of her prescription painkillers—OxyContin, Oxycodone, Xanax, and Neurontin. I would take them in high dosages because they made me feel good. I felt tingly all over, and when my eyes turned into slits, I felt like I was floating. It was like taking acid.

When I told Luis that I was late with my period, he asked me if I was pregnant, so I purchased four home pregnancy tests. One was positive, one was negative, one was positive, and one was negative. I had no clue what to do, and since I didn't know what to do, I kept drinking. And drinking.

Two months passed, and I woke up one morning with excruciating pain in my abdomen. Mom had already left for work. I thought maybe I was getting my period. I got up to go to the bathroom, and that's when I saw blood running down my leg. I had never had a period like that before. By the time I reached the toilet and sat down, a flood of blood poured out of me. That freaked me out. In my dazed state, I didn't realize that I had just had a miscarriage.

I was bleeding profusely, but I did not know what to do. I called Luis, who also freaked out when he came over. He was concerned and said we had to go to his house, where his mother could help us out. When she cleaned me up, she knew right away that it was a miscarriage. "I had two of my own," she said.

I was too embarrassed to tell anyone. I couldn't tell my friends because they would have called me a slut. I couldn't tell my mom because I was fifteen and he was nineteen. The only people I could talk to was Luis, his mother, and his sister. I went home like nothing happened and never discussed what happened with Mom.

The pressure of my miscarriage was too much for our relationship, however. Luis wanted the baby, and he blamed me for losing the child. He said it happened because I had been drinking. It was my fault.

My behavior became really self-destructive at this point. My best friend, Suze, started hanging out with these biker dudes who were around twenty years old. They had a big party one night with seventeen guys and three girls. We were drinking like crazy. I fell asleep and woke up at 5:30 a.m. to a guy with a knife at my throat while he was raping me. I screamed, but there was nothing I could do. The next thing I knew, I woke up and saw Mom. A neighbor friend had told her where I was, and she found me naked on the bed with three guys lying around me. I don't know what happened. Probably all of them raped me.

Within a week or two, I found myself at House of Hope. I had never had God in my life. Whenever I heard the name God, I would curse His name. But I noticed something: the kids had faces that were so peaceful. I immediately felt forgiveness and love and arms reaching out to heaven.

My first Wednesday at House of Hope was spent with the youth group. The people doing the youth ministry explained the Gospel, and when they did an altar call, I walked forward. I figured there had to be something better. Something told me to walk forward.

It's been an amazing change for me. I've learned that I've been forgiven and that life doesn't have to be the way it was. God will never *not* love me, no matter what I do. His Son died for us. He knew we would mess up, but He still sent His son.

These days, I'm three years behind in high school. I'm not going to stress because of it. Whatever I make of my future is what it will be. I'm still a teenager, but now I have a different life, thanks to Christ, and boy, am I thankful.

The Lord our God is merciful and forgiving, even though we have rebelled against him.

—Daniel 9:9, NIV

a boot camp for the soul

keith, fifteen

I started getting into trouble when I was twelve or thirteen. My dad did drugs and stuff, and my brother introduced me to weed. I grew up in a two-parent home, and they were always splitting up. My parents would argue and disagree. Then there were times when I didn't see Dad, who was in and out prison all his life for crimes like forgery and grand theft.

He stole checks from my mom and forged her signature. Can you believe that? He probably had a dozen DUIs. He was a roofer who was always getting fired for not showing up on time to work.

Any time Dad got some money, he would do drugs. Drug paraphernalia was all over the house. Some of my earliest recollections of my father were him rolling joints. One thing I knew: he sure paid a lot more attention to drugs than he did to me or my older brother.

The first time I smoked weed I stole it from my

dad. I took it from his little stash box in his bedroom. I didn't like weed at first, but I still thought it was cool. I soon got used to it because it made me feel relaxed. It helped that everyone I hung out with was doing it, too.

I got in with the wrong crowd. They were a couple of years older than me. They started me drinking liquor like Bacardi rum and Hennessey cognac.

I got into trouble at school. I was a C average student. Sometimes I got an F, but I tried to maintain passing grades. I bounced around different schools. The last one was Excel, one of those opportunity schools where they put all the bad kids together, but that wasn't too smart. I just met more people like me who were messed up on drugs.

Mom yanked me out of the Excel program and started homeschooling me. She had to work, though, and Dad was in jail, and with no one to teach me, I went out and got high with my friends.

When I turned fourteen, things started turning worse. I was smoking and drinking every day of the week and taking pills like Xanex and pain pills. I tried ecstasy—did that four or five times. I sold weed so I could get high and have money in my pocket. I sold to my friends.

I started driving Mom's car when I was thirteen. I would leave late at night and drive around with my buddies, but then the cops caught me at five in the morning. They tried to pull me over, but I jumped on the gas before dumping the car and setting out on foot. They caught me and arrested me.

The authorities were going to send me to state boot camp for two years, but the state attorney let me come to House of Hope because my mom asked them if that would be okay. For a while, I got into trouble, but then I accepted Christ about the first month in. It took a while to sink in, however. I still got in trouble for doing stupid stuff like stealing prescription pills from people. I got in trouble for talking with the girls when I shouldn't have been, so I lost privileges like watching movies or drinking juice. I had to stay in my room a lot.

In my fourth or fifth month, my attitude hadn't changed. My counselors informed me that I could get kicked out and be shipped back to boot camp. I straightened out from there. I didn't want to return to boot camp. It ain't no fun there.

I know it's been a slow process, but I have learned that if I hang out with bad people, they will bring you down. I need to be real with God and strive to live a Christian life.

Drugs will get me nowhere. I realize that now. So does my dad, who found Christ in prison. He had hit rock bottom, but now he's in a Christian program for adults and has stopped doing drugs. He said he was inspired to make a change in his life when he noticed what Christ had done in mine. My dad shows me love now. Our relationship is a lot better.

I am now on home phase at House of Hope. I have chosen different friends, and I hang out with a different crowd. I am making good choices.

Now I am finding out that I can do all things through Christ who strengthens me. I don't plan to get on drugs and fall because now I am high on Jesus.

I can do all things through Christ who strengthens me.

—Philippians 4:13, NKJV

life on the cutting edge

lisa, sixteen

Dad came from a big Italian family that liked to celebrate big, and Dad's way of celebrating was getting drunk and taking drugs. One time on Father's Day, he was driving alone when a cop pulled him over. It was a routine traffic stop until the police officer noticed Dad acting a little suspicious. A car search was conducted, and the cop found a small bag of cocaine.

That was the final straw for Mom. She didn't want that type of husband or that type of father for me, their only child. So she filed for divorce when I was three years old.

I only saw him a few times after the divorce was final. I do remember the time when he called me from jail. That bothered me so much that I cried all night. The last time I ever saw him was on Christmas Eve when I was ten years old. He came by my house with a present, and then he disappeared.

By that time, Mom had met someone else—a cop named Steve. They married, but the honeymoon didn't last long for me. Steve—that's what I called him—was abusive to me, which didn't give me a good impression of what a dad was supposed to be like. Mom and Steve had a baby together right away, but all I remember was their constant verbal fighting, which sometimes turned physical. On one occasion, Steve pinned Mom to the floor and threatened to kill her. She ripped his shirt and put up quite a fight, but Steve continued to sit on her and keep her arms pinned back. Mom screamed for me to call 911, but I was too scared to make the call. The confrontation stopped when a hanging plate fell off the wall and broke.

As I grew up, Steve became more and more abusive. If things didn't go his way, he would take it out on me. He called me names and told me over and over that I would never amount to anything, that I would live in jail like my dad, and that I would end up a loser. We fought continuously, for which I received my share of bruises. One time when we were arguing, Steve pinned me down to my bed and wrapped his big hands around my arms, causing all sorts of bruises.

That was my home life, and it wasn't long before I began looking for love in all the wrong places. I found it in the arms of a seventeen-year-old guy, Jeremy. I was thirteen at the time, but I looked mature for my age. I began smoking weed and doing ecstasy with Jeremy and his friends. He didn't put any sexual pressure on me, but he didn't have to. I wanted to have sex, and lots of it. We used to go to clubs together, and that got me into a sexy party atmosphere.

You may be wondering what my mother thought of all this. She had basically grounded me for life, so to see Jeremy, I snuck out my bedroom window after she went to bed. She had no control over me. After she discovered this, she took the phone out of my room so I couldn't call Jeremy.

I struck back by stealing my grandmother's cell phone, which lasted about a month. It didn't take much detective work for Mom and my grandmother to figure out that all my calls had been dialed to a certain number—the one belonging to my boyfriend. The $300 in cell calls sent Mom through the roof. One day while I was at school, she ransacked my room and found notebooks and letters I had written to my friends describing how Jeremy and I partied, what drugs we took, and how much we were getting it on.

When I arrived home, I found Mom going through all my belongings. I knew my life was over. I cried and carried on all afternoon, and later that evening, I found a steak knife in the kitchen and snuck into my bedroom.

Life wasn't worth living, right? Not with Mom knowing everything. I sat on my bed in the dark, contemplating what had happened. I saw a future without hope, a future that depressed me, so I brought the steak knife above my left wrist and touched the skin. I pressed, lightly at first, but then harder. And then I began moving the knife back and forth across my wrist. Numbness came over me, but instead of feeling excruciating pain, I felt nothing.

I increased the tension and pushed and pushed harder on the knife, moving back and forth, back and forth until blood spurted everywhere. I then put the steak knife in my left hand and attempted to cut the wrist on my right hand, but I couldn't generate any force. I became tired, so tired, and then I fell asleep . . .

At 2 a.m., my mother came into my room to check on me and give me a goodnight kiss. She saw the blood and immediately screamed, "We have to get you to the emergency room right away!"

I was rushed to the ER, where I was sewn up. A parade of doctors stopped by to look at my handiwork. Then I overheard a couple of doctors talking with Mom about sending me to a local mental institution, but she talked them into releasing me into her custody.

Ten days later, I found myself at House of Hope. I can tell you that I was not a happy camper. I was fifteen years old, and although I knew I needed help, I didn't want it at this weird place where they talked about Jesus continually. Perhaps that's because I didn't know much about God. I had only gone to church a few times with my grandparents.

I sat in chapel and looked around. Why was everyone else so happy? So I listened, and I watched, and I saw how God had helped them. This intrigued me. I wanted to know more, and when I came to a place where I was totally broken, I knew I needed Jesus Christ. One month and one day after I arrived at House of Hope, I accepted the Lord.

That happened a year ago. Since then, Psalms 37:4 has become a special verse to me. It says, "Delight yourself in the Lord, and he will give you the desires of your heart." For the first time in my young life, I'm delighting myself in the Lord, and I know He will give me the desires of my heart.

The desire of my heart is to share Christ with people who are lost just like I was. I want to help those who are hurting, probably because there was a time when my life hurt so much, I wanted to end it.

This year, I am traveling to Women of Faith conferences with Miss Sara. I am speaking to thousands of women, sharing my testimony, giving hope to those who are hurting and telling them that Jesus is the answer to healing broken lives.

Commit your way to the Lord; trust in him and he will do this: He will make your righteousness shine like the dawn, and the justice of your cause like the noonday sun.

—Psalms 37: 5-6, NIV

transported to a different heavenly world

megan, seventeen

I grew up in Buford, South Carolina, where my father served in the Marine Corps, but my parents divorced when I was two years old. At first, I was passed back and forth between my dad and mom, but then they sent me to my grandparents in California when I was three. Mom had her issues because she was diagnosed with an anxiety disorder, but I was returned to her when I was six. We lived in Orlando, and a couple of years later, she got married and got pregnant right away. Shortly after my sister Kaitlin arrived, my stepfather committed suicide. That made my mom's anxiety really bad.

She stayed in her bedroom all day. She didn't have to work because she got money from the life insurance, plus an inheritance following her father's death. When my real father found out how neglected I was, he said he didn't want me living with her anymore. He had me move to Daytona with him and his live-in girlfriend, Laurie. She raised me and took good care of me, and life got better for a while. In sixth grade, though, we moved to Orlando, where Dad worked long hours as a traffic controller. I got in with the wrong crowd at school and tried marijuana for the first time. Meanwhile, Laurie left Dad because he didn't want her to become a flight attendant.

Laurie tried to keep in contact with me after she moved out, but Dad didn't like that. I was left to raise myself since Dad was never home. I started smoking a lot of marijuana and drinking in the ninth grade. When marijuana got boring, I tried ecstasy, which I fell in love with. Ecstasy took me out of everything and transported me into a heaven world. The best part was that I got it for free. A neighbor of mine, a sixteen-year-old boy, would give it to me, so I started having sex with him.

Meanwhile, Dad got a new girlfriend named Lisa. Since he was always at her place when he got off work, I had our house all to myself. I started throwing these huge parties. One Saturday night, one hundred kids came over, and things really got out of hand. I retreated to my bedroom totally out of it. I could still hear people partying downstairs, getting high, playing PlayStation, and music blasting throughout the house. The pungent aroma of marijuana rose up to my second-floor bedroom.

You need only one ecstasy pill to get you high, and two or three can kill you, but I kept popping them one after another down my throat until I had swallowed *thirteen.* I don't know what I was thinking, but then I began "rolling," which means that the ecstasy really grabbed a hold of me. I felt as though I was going into a trance. Then I turned and saw a Bible on my dresser—the Bible that my grandmother had given me. It was just a room decoration, but that evening, I thought if I just held the Bible, then something good might happen. I kept asking myself, *Why am I doing this?*

I cried out, "God, I know it's you."

This is not what I have planned for you, I felt Him tell me in my heart.

"Take me out of this," I wailed.

The next thing I remember is my father shaking me the next morning. "What are you doing?" he said. "What's going on? Wake up."

I struggled to focus my eyes. That's when I noticed a guy laying next to me in the bed. *How did he get there?* I didn't know what had happened.

"Who are the other people sleeping in the house?" Dad demanded.

Other people? Dad started screaming, "Have you been doing drugs? Are you high?"

I said no.

"Then what's this?" he asked, pointing to a weed bag stuck to my shoulder.

I'm so done, I thought. Dad kicked everyone out of the house. Then he brought me to a doctor's office, where I was given a drug test and a physical. I was so embarrassed. When we were finished, Dad drove me to House of Hope. My first appointment was with Miss Sandy, one of the staff. She studied me and then said, "You're not happy, are you?"

"No," I mumbled.

"Do you need to stay here for a while?"

It was the right question at the right time. "Yes, I need to be here," I said as I started crying. Miss

Sandy hugged me and prayed for me to receive Jesus in my heart. Now I was bawling. I just knew everything would get better.

Everything has gotten better. Dad has remarried and has a baby. Laurie, who I still keep in contact with, became a Southwest Airlines flight attendant and is getting married. You see, when I said a prayer, God totally listened. He moved me out of a bad situation and fixed everything. It if weren't for the Lord, I probably wouldn't be here. God is so good.

I'm going to do homeschooling and get a high school diploma as I wait on the Lord to see what He has in store for me. God hasn't confirmed anything for me yet, but I know that whatever I do, it will be serving the Lord. I never thought God would give me the opportunity to speak to mothers and teenagers. Miss Sara takes me with her to speak at Women of Faith conferences. So many teens and mothers are hurting . . . they come to me for comfort. I always encourage the mothers and grandmothers to spend lots of time with their children. I know what it's like to not have a mother there for me. That has been very hurtful.

We all go through hurtful things. No matter what your struggles, please give God a chance. You can't do it on your own. He will be right there for you. Don't be ashamed to ask for help. God will change your heart when you give Him your will.

Forgetting what is behind and straining toward what is ahead, I press on toward the goal to win the prize for which God has called me heavenward in Christ Jesus.

—Philippians 3:13b-14, NIV

running up bills

michelle, fourteen

When I was three years old, I was adopted. Five years later, Mom had her car accident. She and a friend were driving on company time to a meeting when their car hit a ditch in the middle of a country road. Mom broke her neck, and though she wasn't paralyzed, she wound up with two herniated disks and a bulging disk in her neck.

Mom was out of work for three or four months. Meanwhile, she got all a bunch of credit cards and maxed them out on clothes, gold necklaces, gold earrings, makeup, shoes and whatever else shopaholics buy. I can remember her taking me to the mall on weekends, and we would buy out the stores. Mom bought me anything I wanted, but perhaps that's because I was an only child. When Dad started noticing the mountain of credit card bills coming in, he asked her where she had gotten the credit cards. They had an agreement that she wouldn't get credit cards. Dad told Mom that had lied to him, so he announced that he wanted a divorce.

This greatly unsettled me. I lived in a weird house anyway. My mom was a Christian and sang with the worship team at church, but my dad didn't care about God. I sometimes played hooky from church because I thought I could since Dad didn't go.

Meanwhile, Mom had sued her company because of the accident, and the settlement more than covered the run-up in credit card bills. She and Dad—who had decided to withdraw the divorce action—purchased a new home and each got new cars: a Jeep for him and a Hyundai Sonata for her. Mom knew that this settlement was a once-in-a-lifetime windfall, so she learned her lesson and cut up her credit cards.

She still had enough money leftover to spoil me, however. Mom continued to buy me clothes and jewelry, as well as to get me massages and my hair and nails done. I became a good shopper, too. I was also a good dancer since Mom had put me in lessons since I was two years old. I knew how to do tap, ballet, modern, hip hop, lyrical—I took lessons three to four times a week. My favorite was jazz dancing, which is a mixture of ballet and hip-hop and very upbeat.

I'm not sure why, but when I turned eleven years old, I became very rebellious. Maybe it was because I was still worried that my parents would follow through with the divorce. But if my mom asked me to clean my room, I'd yell no back and stomp off and ignore her.

When I turned twelve, I did something really

stupid: I had sex with my best friend's cousin to find out what it was like. He was sixteen. I think I wanted to lose my virginity because I heard so much about sex at school. It was sung about a lot in the music I listened to, and the TV shows were always about sex. So I wanted to find out what everyone was talking about.

Three weeks later, my best friend Amber was over at my house. Sometime around 12:30 in the morning, we snuck out my bedroom window and walked forty-five minutes to these guys' house. We knew one of the boys, who was twelve, but we wanted to hang with his older brother, who was nineteen. Several of his friends were over when we arrived. Their mom was apparently spending the night at her boyfriend's house.

Jimmy, the nineteen-year-old, motioned me to the back bedroom. I followed him, and we started talking a bit.

Then he cut to the chase. "Do you want to have sex with me?" he asked.

"Ah, gee, I don't know," I said. I was scared and nervous, and I didn't know what to do.

"It's okay, nothing bad is going to happen to you."

"If it's okay, I'd rather not," I said. We continued talking, and about a half-hour later, we stepped back out into the living room, where my friend Amber was lying on the floor, drunk and passed out.

I shook her awake and said we had to go. It was 3 a.m., and we had to get home before Dad got up to go to work. We had no sooner snuck back in, gotten into bed, when Mom got up and checked on us. We held our breath and pretended to sleep. We had just made it!

My rebellious attitude extended to school as well. I developed a reputation for my outbursts in school. If my teacher asked me to do something, I'd yell at him or her. Once I hit my teacher because he wouldn't let me go to the bathroom. That got me into trouble, but I didn't like authority. "Shut up!"

I would yell when I stormed out of the classroom. "I don't care what you're trying to get me to do."

When Mom heard about this, she had had enough. She sent me to a private Christian school for the eighth grade, where I noticed that many of my classmates were from my old middle school. I did a little better in the classroom, but I was still disrespectful.

I had an aunt who was really cool. She liked to smoke marijuana with me, and I could tell her everything—including sneaking out and having premarital sex. When I turned fourteen, I met this twenty-five-year-old guy, and he would give me weed and wads of money. One time, he drove over to my aunt's house, and my aunt and I walked out to the car and got in to smoke a couple of joints with him. After laughing and giggling for a while, my aunt went back to the house; she had a husband and two children waiting for her. I stayed in the car and had sex in the back seat with him.

I spent the night at my aunt's house. The next morning, my aunt and my uncle took me out to breakfast, where she proceeded to tell her husband about everything. My uncle was my mom's brother, so he told my mom everything. Mom confronted me and then basically grounded me for life. I couldn't do anything or talk to anybody.

During the summer before my ninth grade, Mom announced she had found a residential home where she wanted me to be interviewed. It was called House of Hope, she said.

We met with Miss Sara, but I thought we were there to check it out. Wrong. I was staying.

I did not like it. I had a big attitude. For several days, I didn't talk to anyone. The walls went up, but slowly, I began talking to my counselor about everything. She said I had to get used to humbling myself, and that was a foreign concept to me. Then as I heard the Gospel presented to me, I began learning what true humility was all about. Jesus Christ humbled Himself when He came on this earth.

But what really sealed the deal for me was meeting with Pastor Frank in his office one day. He explained very calmly and very rationally that there is a heaven and a hell, and I had the choice to go to either of them. *Hmmm.* I knew I was on the track to hell. I didn't want to go to hell for the rest of eternity. As Pastor Frank pointed out, all those who have Christ in their lives are promised salvation and will spend eternity with Him in heaven. Those who don't . . . they go to hell.

Some people find that concept stark, but it's clear in my mind. I accepted Christ shortly afterward in a chapel setting. I had been at House of Hope for five or six months. I know that's a little longer than most people here, but I was a tougher nut.

Sometimes you can be too stubborn. I've learned

my lesson the hard way. If you are a know-it-all like I was, I can save you a lot of pain if you'll pray the prayer I did:

Dear Lord Jesus,

I can't do it on my own. I keep making mistakes. I need Your help. Please forgive me for my bad choices. Please come into my heart as my Lord and Savior.

In Your precious name. Amen.

And being found in appearance as a man, he [Jesus] humbled himself and became obedient to death—even death on a cross!

—Philippians 2:8, NIV

looking for a touch

ryan, seventeen

After my parents got divorced when I was in sixth grade, I started getting into drugs. I skipped class to smoke weed with my friends or do whatever I felt like. When I was in the classroom, I was always trying to get my teacher mad. If she said, "Ryan, sit down and take notes," I ignored her and told another one of my stupid jokes.

My grades sank. My report card was filled with Cs, Ds, and incompletes, so I basically gave up on school. I didn't see any need for it or any reason to try. No one was there for me. Mom worked a lot and was never around.

That happened all through middle school, but during my freshman year, I started drinking and popping pills. Everything fell apart for me in tenth grade. I would attend one class period and then walk off campus and hop in my friend's car. The school authorities didn't care. They never called my mom to tell her that I was ditching class. Then I came home one day to see some cops in my front yard looking up a tree.

"We're looking for a raccoon," one of the cops said.

We didn't expect to have cops in my front yard when we drove up. One of my friends had a gram of weed in a baggie sticking out of his back pocket.

"Well, what do we have here?" said a cop.

They searched us and found another gram in my pocket. This landed me in a juvenile detox center, where they send kids for several days until they get clean. Apparently, the cops had been on to my friends and me, and the raccoon chase was bogus. The court ordered me to attend a Level II state program, which was like going to school, but they made sure we attended every class, and they drug-tested us at least once a week. The ironic thing is that I found more drugs at this Level II program than at my old regular school.

Meanwhile, Mom started dating a guy in construction who she thought wasn't doing drugs anymore. J.J. swore to Mom that he was an ex-alcoholic and ex-druggie, so they lived together and then got married. He needed some help at the construction site, and I needed some money, so I began helping him out. One day, I said, "I need to smoke," referring to weed, and I said that because I just knew that he needed to smoke some weed, too. After that, he started buying me alcohol before he introduced me to crack. I hadn't tried crack before, but he let me smoke some of it out of a bowl. I liked smoking it.

I continued to attend the Level II program, but one day I flipped out at the teacher. I got so mad that I punched a hole in the wall. The cops were called, and they re-assessed the usefulness of that state-run program. I was only supposed to be there five months, but after nine months, I hadn't moved up one of the five phases. They said this place wasn't working for me, so I had to go to some type of residential program.

My mom didn't want me to go into another state-run program. She wanted a Christian program for me, and when a friend told her about House of Hope, I was on my way.

House of Hope is a residential program, of course, which angered me. I had always lived in the same house since I was four months old. I liked that stability, so I despised coming to House of Hope.

But that's what I had to do, so I decided to make the most of it. A couple of months after coming here, I was sitting in chapel, barely paying attention while everyone was praying and worshipping. Something moved me, so I prayed to God that evening. I said, "If you are really there God, you have to touch me right now."

Two seconds after I made that statement, I felt a touch on my shoulder. It was another guy in the program. "You should follow me and come up to the front," he said, so that I could get some prayer and counseling from the preacher.

Hmmm. I stood up and followed my friend forward, thinking, "Thank you, God, for showing me a sign. Now I know you're really there."

Then I asked Jesus to come into my heart, and I asked Him to forgive me for everything I had done. After I prayed that prayer, I started getting tingly and began shaking. I think God was getting all the bad stuff out of me, all the demons out. After that day, I never doubted God. I always knew He was there. I never questioned Him.

Although I had become a Christian, change did not happen overnight. I remember sneaking out of my house at House of Hope and smoking some cigarettes with some other guys. After we came back from Christmas break, the guys and I came together and said we had to stop doing that. Some of us took it a step further. Josh and I confessed everything we did to the counselors, who dropped us from second phase to first phase. At House of Hope, we have five phases before we pass the program: orientation, first phase, second phase, third phase, home phase, and graduation.

With a renewed commitment to God, I began moving up in phases rapidly. I started reading the Bible as much as I could. I was hungry for God. I read the Gospels and some of Acts.

Now that I'm back on the right track, I would definitely say the only reason things have turned around for me is because of God and the great work He has started in me.

When I was a child, I talked like a child, I thought like a child, I reasoned like a child. When I became a man, I put childish ways behind me.

—1 Corinthians 13:11, NIV

a good match all the way around

amber, sixteen

My mom was nineteen years when she became pregnant with me. She had no boyfriend and no money. Thank God she didn't abort me, but after I was born, we had to live with my grandparents in Savannah, Georgia.

My grandparents watched me while Mom went to work. I was a happy kid. I liked to run around, climb trees, and eat bugs. Grandpa would take me fishing a lot since we lived on a river. It was something fun to do.

When I was in fourth grade, Mom met and married Gary. We moved into an apartment and got a dog. They worked a lot, so I would go to my grandparents' house after school because they lived close to us.

I was in fifth grade when a friend who lived down the street introduced me to pot. She was a cool seventh grader. I was so dumb. I failed a lot of classes in fifth grade because I smoked every day, but my parents never knew. One time, we broke into a house down the street just for something to do. Because I was doing so poorly in school, my parents decided to homeschool me. They could do this because they worked the night shift. Mom worked at a Safeway, and Dad worked at Target.

We moved to Destin, Florida, which is a big vacation place for spring break, and Mom sent me back to public school in seventh grade. It was so boring. I didn't like to do anything. I didn't like the people that much. I thought everything was so corrupt, like it was all lies. I could see the negative part of everything, which made me more and more depressed. Then my grandpa died, which sent me into a deeper funk. It proved how everything sucks.

Going into ninth grade, I had several good friends named Alissa, Jenna, Rebecca, and Phoebe. They also happened to be my only friends. We dyed our hair purple, spiked our hair, and we wore spikes on our arms and baggy clothes and chains. Not many people dressed like that in Destin, which made us real outsiders. The rednecks at school were so mean. They spit on us. They called us freaks and dykes.

We got back at them. We shot food coloring into their lockers, and we put dead mice, dead fish, and lizards with their heads cut off in their lockers. We blew up pictures of people we didn't like and taped them to our shirts with the inscription, "I Love Joe Don" on it. During election week, we wrote the "Biggest Fag Award" for one of the guys running for class president. On another, we wrote, "Vote for Curtis, Twinkie President of the World." Curtis, who was overweight, must have eaten a lot of Twinkies.

We were little anarchists. I didn't believe in anarchy, but our school was like an awful prison. We got tired of being hassled by the rednecks. There was one particular girl who wanted to kill me. She would e-mail these nasty hate letters, saying that she wanted to poison my food. We took our aggression out at metal concerts, where my friends and I slugged others as we jumped around in the mosh pit. Those metalheads never knew what hit them.

Living like this got me so depressed. I started to cut myself and pierce myself with safety pins. I kind of liked the pain because it was such a release. I cut myself on my arms, legs, and stomach with scissors and razors. I bled and got scars. Another thing we would do was brand ourselves with our rings. We would heat up our rings until they were really hot and then brand ourselves on the arm or the stomach. It didn't hurt. It was cool.

One of my best friends was Alissa, who also lived with her grandparents. After her grandma died, she said, "Hey, let's get our grandparents hooked up."

We planned it out great. I got my grandma to take me to Olive Garden, and Alissa arrived with her grandpa just as we put our names in for a table.

"Hey, Alissa, it's so good to see you," I said, as I hugged her. "Hey Grandma, can Alissa and her grandfather sit with us? It would be so much fun."

We did have a lot of fun, and our little matchmaking plan worked. Alissa's grandpa asked Grandma to marry him a few months later, and now my best friend is also my cousin. That is so cool.

As for my romantic front, I had always dated guys and always used guys. We didn't go all the way, but we almost did. It was in tenth grade, though, that I started having real sex. I would sneak out at night and go to the guy's house for a few hours. Then I got a job at TCBY, the frozen yogurt place, working the late shift. I worked with this guy whose friend, a drug dealer, would come by just before we closed at 12:30. The drug dealer would weigh all his drugs on our scales to find out how much he had sold that night, and then he would give me some for my trouble. "You're a cute kid," he would say.

He usually gave me some crip, a form of enhanced pot. We would go smoke in the freezer so we didn't smell up the place. They gave me so much. I would come home late at 12:30, go to sleep for a couple of hours, wake up at 2:30 with my alarm, and leave and hang out with my friends. I would smoke some more drugs and come back at 5 a.m., when I would go to sleep until 7 o'clock and go to school.

I somehow managed to keep up with my homework because I didn't work or sneak out every night. But one time I was over at my boyfriend's house, and his dad walked in on us at 5 a.m. It was obvious that we had been having sex and doing drugs.

My parents said that was it—I had to go into a program. So I ran away and stayed with friends for two weeks until my parents found me. Then they packed up some of my belongings, drove us to Orlando, and put me into House of Hope.

I was given a room with three other girls. "Are you a good girl or a bad girl?" one asked me shortly after I arrived.

That was a good question. I changed the subject. "Can I pierce you guys?" I asked, as I took out a safety pin. "It's like an awesome relief."

"Yes, we'll try it," said one.

I did three other girls, and we got caught, and we got dropped a level for discipline. And then it dawned on me: if I keep getting put on discipline, I'll never get home. As for where God fit in my life, I believed in Him and all that, but I never liked Him because of what other people did to me, and I blamed Him.

I started to think about God more and more. I didn't accept Christ in the first month or two like many kids do at House of Hope. I didn't want to be like everyone else and accept Christ at a chapel or with a counselor. I said to myself that I'll get there someday, but I'll do it myself. I was a little rebel.

About six months passed when I went home on a weekend pass. I was in church back in Destin with my parents. They had started going to church, and I could see something had changed in them.

I went to church with them, and when their pastor explained the Gospel, I sat there thinking. I didn't want to be depressed any longer. I was tired of cutting myself. I didn't want to hate my parents. I stood up and went forward when they had an altar call. I was ready—more than ready.

I love church now. It's cool.

I think I have a cool future ahead of me. I'm happy, and I'm content. The Bible verse on the next page says it all: I thought I could do what I want, but all along, I was headed down the wrong path.

Now I'm going in a better direction. My advice to

you is don't do something because it feels right or seems right. Be sure your actions are pleasing to God.

There is a way that seems right to a man, but in the end, it leads to death.

—Proverbs 16:25, NIV

restoring what the locusts had taken away

gabriel, fourteen

My mom was a foot taller than my father, who was five feet, five inches tall and born in Belize. Mom, who was of Puerto Rican descent with the looks of a supermodel, stood six-foot, five inches tall.

All I can remember is that they constantly fought when I grew up. One time Mom threw a ten-speed bike at Dad, who deflected it with his arm and then took her to divorce court. I was in first grade when they split up.

Mom told me I wouldn't be seeing Daddy anymore, and that bothered me. I started getting into trouble in school with a whole bunch of referrals. One time I threw a chair at my teacher. (I would have thrown a bike if there was one in the classroom.) I set a new record for referrals with twenty-four, breaking the old record of twelve. Each time I visited with the principal, I received an ISS, which was an in-school suspension (that meant I had to stay in a classroom and work all day) or an OSS, an out-of-school suspension that was a one-way ticket to stay home for the day. I got a lot of those.

I had one older brother and a couple of younger sisters. My grandma watched us when we came home from school because Mom was a business-woman who often stayed late at the office. I don't know what was keeping her at the office until one or three in the morning, but I did know that a lot of guys liked her. Mom was also into drugs.

When I was in third grade, she met a man named Enrique who was an abusive drinker and not well kept. He wanted to marry Mom. He proposed to her one day, but she turned him down cold. He had a daughter from a previous marriage, and she could tell that he would be bad news.

Enrique still came by the house every now and then to see Mom, but she moved on. Mom met a new guy who could get upset in a hurry. He exploded on my mother for the littlest thing. I think she took this abuse out on me. I was always the child in the family who took the beating. Mom would hit me across the face, or she would take one of those big construction worker belts, a thick leather one, and whip me with it. I always got a whipping after one of those referrals or when I came home with bad grades.

One day Enrique, Mom's old boyfriend, asked my grandmother if he could get a key to the house. He said he wanted to surprise my mother by cooking dinner for us one night. One evening—I was in the fourth grade at the time—I woke up in the middle of the night. Sometimes when that happened, I tiptoed into Mom's bedroom and crawled in her bed. I liked sleeping next to Mom because she was my mom.

On this occasion, I fell asleep in Mom's bed only to be awakened by Enrique in the middle of the night. He had used the key to get into the house. When he walked into the bedroom, he startled us. When Mom asked him what he was doing there, he told me to leave.

I left the bedroom, but I left the door a tiny bit ajar. I peaked in and watched Enrique start gesturing and waving his arms toward Mom. He said things like, "If I can't have you, then nobody can." They started wrestling with each other. Then he pulled out a handgun, and I watched in horror as he shot my mom in the head.

Enrique never knew that I watched him drag Mom's body to the floor, where he stuffed her body half under the bed. He lay down on top of her with his head on her chest. Then he put the gun to his forehead and pulled the trigger.

I thought the horror that I had just witnessed was a bad dream. I returned to my bedroom like a zombie and fell back asleep. My siblings and I woke up in the morning as we normally did, and we had this routine. We would watch TV until Mom woke up, cooked us breakfast, got us dressed, and drove us off to school.

On this morning, however, we watched TV . . . and more TV . . . and more TV. Around nine a.m., we knocked on her bedroom door. No answer. Then my brother found a note on the carpet. It was from Enrique. It said:

Kids.
Mommy is sick.
I am sick.
Call Grandma.
Enrique

We called Grandma, and when she arrived, we opened the bedroom door and were horrified to find blood everywhere. Grandma screamed and told me to call 911. The crime scene was absolutely shocking. It didn't seem real.

The homicide department arrived, and we were questioned one by one. I was confused. I thought everything was a bad dream. I didn't tell anyone that I had witnessed the murder-suicide. Within a few days, the authorities eventually found my father, and the four of us went to live with him and my other grandmother for a year.

I soon got kicked out of my new school for bad behavior. I was sent to an ESC school—one for emotionally scarred children. I had anger issues and still got in trouble. In the fifth grade, I started getting into gangs in the Orlando area. I was too young to be a gang member, but the Bloods and the Crips and the LKs let me hang around and do little chores for them, like steal stuff. I wasn't an official member of the gang, but I'll never forget the time a gang leader stuck a loaded gun into my face and said I had to do what he told me to do.

Meanwhile, Dad had remarried, and now I had a stepmom. Because all my anger, I snapped on her one day, so badly that the cops came and they took me to a facility for kids with mental problems.

My parents found out about House of Hope and put me into a once-a-week counseling program. During one Tuesday night program, I heard the Gospel presented, and I asked Jesus to come into my life. Not long after that, I became a full-time resident. Initially, I got into trouble with anger and disrespecting authority, but I never ran away.

One Sunday morning I sat down in the church that House of Hope took us to that day, and the pastor said if something has been eating you, that if you need to get right with God, then come to the altar and renew your faith. Ever since then, I feel as though I have really turned a corner. Sure, I still stumble, and we all go through tribulation, but I've placed my trust in the Lord and am sure that He will use me for His great plan.

I really feel that Jesus can restore what the locusts have eaten, which is my Bible verse. There was a locust inside me, eating my heart and keeping me from God. When I lifted my heart to Him, He restored that huge hole inside me and filled it with His love.

Just in case you're hurting like I was, and you feel you have a hole inside your heart, will you pray this prayer with me?

Jesus, I trust You to heal that hurt in me . . . will You please bring someone into my life who will share God's love with me like You did for Gabriel?

In Your precious name. Amen.

I will repay you for the years the locusts have eaten—the great locust and the young locust, the other locusts and the locust swarm—my great army that I sent among you.

You will have plenty to eat, until you are full, and you will praise the name of the Lord your God, who has worked wonders for you; never again will my people be shamed. Then you will know that I am in Israel, that I am the Lord your God, and that there is no other; never again will my people be shamed.

—Joel 2;25-27, NIV

fearfully and wonderfully made

chelsea, seventeen

My story begins when I started taking dancing classes at three years of age in Coon Rapids, a Minneapolis suburb. My mom really invested in dance, driving me to practice seven days a week while I was schooled in ballet, tap, jazz, salsa—everything. By the time I was in elementary school, I was dancing four to six hours a day. My teachers said that I was such a natural that I probably came out of Mom's womb doing the splits.

My teachers used to call me Gumby. I was a contortionist who could put my legs behind my head or lay on my stomach and touch my toes to my nose. People could bend me into a human hula-hoop or scrunch me up like a backpack.

Mom dreamed of me becoming a professional ballerina. I think that's because she had the same dream when she was young, but her parents didn't let her dance because they thought it was satanic or something. That's silly. Dancing isn't evil—it's an art form. Nevertheless, Mom pushed me into the studio and thought I would be on Broadway some day.

When I turned ten, I won the first of seventeen scholarships, or free trips, to Los Angeles dance studios, where I learned from some of Hollywood's top professionals. I usually housed with families on these two-week trips to Southern California and danced ten hours a day. I auditioned for movies and talent agencies, and I even got into one movie, but it was never distributed. I liked being on center stage. I had no problem performing in front of thousands. I did not shrink from the limelight—I was attracted to it.

Right after I turned fourteen, my parents were divorced. I moved with my mom to another town about forty-five minutes away. It seems that when we made that move, I didn't want to dance any more. Maybe that's because I had done it year-round since I was three years old. Whatever the reason, I suddenly went from being a willing dancer to someone who told my mom flat-out: "There's no way I'm getting in that car and going to dance class."

Mom wasn't happy with the news, but she couldn't force me. She could still get in her little digs, though. Whenever I said I was going to McDonald's with my friends or looking in the refrigerator for a snack, she could come up with comments like, "No more fries, thunderthighs," or "That cookie is loaded with fat grams. Eat a piece of celery." She said this even though I had no problem with weight: at five feet, seven inches, I weighed 110 pounds.

This was when I entered what Mom called my "demon child" stage. I started skipping school, smoking pot, and drinking beer and hard liquor. My grandma was living with us and thought dancing was satanic, and she was so abusive to me. One time she was chasing me around and beating me. I ran up the stairs, but she kept coming after me, so I gave her a head butt, and she tumbled down the stairs just like they do in the movies. She called the cops.

Before the police arrived, I grabbed my backpack and jumped out my bedroom window and ran down to Jessica's house. That's where the cops found me. I was driven to my father's house to cool down. I'll never forget what the cop said to me: "You'll be pregnant in three months," he said, "just like your sister." My seventeen-year-old sister had gotten pregnant by her boyfriend.

The only thing I had going at school was being on the dance line—kind of like a competitive dance team. We performed at football and basketball games. Then I got kicked out for showing up drunk one time. I figured after that I might as well start hanging out with the bad kids since the dance line kids didn't like me. In fact, they hated me. I got the worst looks in school from them.

I started doing crystal methamphetamine—known as "glass"—with my new friends. The second that I snorted glass, I was addicted. I told the boys that if they got me high, I would do stuff with them, but I was such a tease. Every three-inch line of glass literally puts a hole in your brain. Not only does glass totally deteriorate your brain, it can burn straight through your skin or ruin your teeth enamel because it's made with some ingredients like ammonia, Drano and cocaine. If you get it on your gums, your teeth will rot. I remember one of my friends had perfect teeth until he did glass; two of his incisor teeth rotted out.

I fell in love with my dealer, a guy named Jeff who was twenty-six years old. He had the sense to know that a twenty-six-year-old guy and a sixteen-year-old girl were not a good match, but I waited by the phone for him. He had uses for me, though. Since I looked like the biggest prep in the crowd, he had me make his deliveries and pick up drugs for him.

Shortly after my sister had her baby, I did glass for two weeks straight—no sleep, and no eating. I was such an actress. I would come home at five or six in the morning and act like I had been home all night, but I wouldn't need to sleep because I was on drugs.

I eventually became so delusional, however, that I started overdosing at home. My brother called 911, and the cops and paramedics came. I was stabilized, and the paramedics thought I could go with the cops to Juvenile Detention.

While I was locked up, I was in such bad shape that I licked some glass residue off my creases in my hands. This destroyed my taste buds. For the next six months or so, I passed through a series of residential programs—twelve in all. I went through every secular program, psych ward, and drug rehab center that could be found. None of them worked.

Meanwhile, my grandparents had moved to Florida, where they heard of House of Hope. Mom gave them guardianship, and off I went.

When I arrived at House of Hope, I thought I could act my way out of this program, too. But I soon learned that I had a new audience watching me—Jesus Christ. Maybe I could fool the house staff at House of Hope, but I couldn't fool God who saw all things and knew my every thought.

One time at a chapel service, Pastor Frank was talking about the plan God has for our lives, and God gave me a vision of life in a dark room where everything was black, white, or gray. The only thing that made color in the room was God's light shining through the window. That was it for me. Suddenly, my life had color, and I felt this immense comfort and peace.

I knew I needed to accept Christ into my heart. I approached Pastor Frank after the service and said, "I have to get saved."

Pastor Frank laughed. He said he had something he had to do, but that he would come over to my house that night to pray with me.

When I got to my house, I waited and waited for him, and then I didn't want to wait any longer. I said to myself, *I have to get saved tonight.* I needed to feel whole. So I closed my eyes and imagined this old man, balding and with gray hair, sitting in a meadow. I was a little kid, and I ran into his lap and jumped in. "Daddy, please help me," I prayed. "I need you."

All of the sudden, my heart just melted and felt so warm inside. All the pieces came together.

Since I made a decision to believe in God, I have to admit that I still struggle. I have forgiven my mom and dad for the problems between us. I have forgiven my grandparents, who used to hit me. I have made a choice to forgive, and my heart is healing.

Today I'm living a life without dance, without drugs, and without boys, and I don't mean to be conceited, but I know that I am truly fearfully and wonderfully made. My life is now focused on things that will last forever, not on today's feelings that could get me in trouble.

If I could give you some advice to keep you from suffering like I did, I would tell you to look to God to fulfill every need, for He is faithful if you ask. And He will never disappoint you. Everything from God is good!

For you created my inmost being; you knit me together in my mother's womb. I praise you because I am fearfully and wonderfully made.

—Psalms 139:13-14a, NIV

money can't buy me love

bryan, sixteen

I grew up in a lonely home. Both of my parents worked in military contracting, which meant lots of overtime. I never saw them. They rushed out the front door at 7 a.m., and they usually didn't return home until eight or nine o'clock at night. They often worked Saturdays and Sundays. Whenever Mom departed on a business trip, she returned home with several toys she had purchased, usually action figures like Indians or G.I. Joes. That was Mom, always trying to buy my love.

I was left in the care of my brother Aaron, who was seven years older than me. He would walk with me to the private Christian school that we attended, and he watched out for me, almost like a father. We were best friends until he graduated from high school and enlisted in the Air Force as an armor specialist—the guy who puts Cruise missiles and deadly bombs on planes.

At twelve years of age, my guardian and protector

was gone. I needed friends, so I started to hang out with several guys in my class. If one of them wore something cool, I made sure Mom bought me the same thing at the mall. Like I said, Mom liked buying things for me. That showed her love. At fourteen, my cool friends began smoking cigarettes and marijuana. I did, too.

Dad had just retired, but he was a really introverted guy around the house. He liked to tinker in the garage and then kick back and watch TV. We had TVs everywhere in the house, including the kitchen, the back patio, and every bedroom. He wasn't a big sports watcher, unless there was a boxing match on ESPN. Otherwise, he was transfixed by A&E autobiographies and shows on the History Channel.

Dad wasn't a happy guy; for whatever reason, he became physically and verbally abusive with me. He came from a melting pot background. His parents were Indonesian, but he was born and raised in the Netherlands, so he grew up speaking Indonesian, Dutch, Vietnamese, Spanish, French, and English. But his favorite language to yell at me was in Dutch.

"You're stupid!" he'd scream, on the occasions he chastised me in English. "You're never going to amount to anything if you slack off. You're lazy." I thought everyone my age went through this abuse, and I just had to get through it. Since yelling was all I heard around the house, I got angry when my dad raised his voice at me.

Dad had served in the U.S. military in the Sixties, including a tour of duty in Vietnam where he was a prisoner of war. Let's just say that he knew how to handle himself, and when he got mad, he knocked me on the ground. Frequently he would explode in a fury, punch me in the mouth, and smack my glasses off. Another favorite move was kicking me in the back of the leg, which caused me to drop to the floor in pain.

Then he'd apologize for losing his cool. I was just a kid trying to figure out what was happening, but I started picking up some basics when it came to fighting. I became pretty good at holding my own at school. I was the loner type anyway, so if someone challenged me, I spoke with my fists.

I began getting into many fights at school. In the sixth grade, I took on eighth graders and ninth graders—and I took them out. One time, I did a one-punch knockout to a kid because he was picking on me. As I wrestled him to the ground and began pummeling him, a male teacher jumped on my back. I spun around and punched him. That was my last fight at the private Christian school I attended; I was expelled after that.

In public school, I chose to eat lunch alone because I didn't trust anybody. Slowly, I was drawn to other loners on campus. We liked doing drugs together. You name it, we tried it. I liked lacing my weed with coke. By the ninth grade, I began hanging with some gang guys. From the outside, they looked like family to me. They said if I wanted to be in, I could join. They belonged to the Gutta Fam gang, a branch of the Crips, made up of mostly brown kids like me. I was the product of my dad, who was a fairly dark-skinned Indonesian, and my mom, who was white. I looked like the Puerto Rican kids in the gang.

By age fifteen or so, I had filled out. I wasn't tall—five feet, nine inches—but I was ripped. I played football in high school, and I liked playing linebacker because I could hit people. To join Gutta Fam, though, I had to prove my mettle. They told me for my initiation, I would have to jump somebody and get in trouble for it. I said that was cool. I wanted to belong to a family in the worst way, so I jumped this kid in school and put him in the hospital. What a rush!

It wasn't long before I had a bad rep in Orlando. I moved up the ladder pretty quickly and became the No. 2 guy, right under the OG—the person who runs that branch of the gang. My OG—which stands for "Original Gangster"—was a twenty-three-year-old from New York City, and he respected me. Soon, I had plenty of money in my pocket, and with money, I could have any girl I wanted. I became sexually active in a big way.

Now, you may be wondering where were my parents in all this. They never had a clue. I put on such a front to my parents. They thought I was an angel kid. They believed me when I said I was staying at a friend's house, and they never questioned why I was gone for days at a time. Whenever I did go home, Mom would give me money because she still wanted to spoil me. If she handed me a $20 bill, I would buy some drugs from a wholesaler and resell them at a profit. Then I had enough cash to take a girl out and have sex with her afterward. That's how it worked.

I noticed that on the few occasions when I was home, Dad wasn't yelling at me so much. Then he dropped the bomb that he and Mom were looking at a divorce, but he didn't want one. In fact, he said he'd kill himself if she went through with it.

One night, Dad and I watched some boxing on TV, and I got up to leave. I wanted to visit my girlfriend and have sex with her, so I said I would be staying at a friend's house.

"It's best that way," he said, which sounded funny to me. Then Dad said another strange thing as I left. "I love you," he said.

"Right," I grunted, but I didn't say "I love you" back.

The next morning, my uncle called and said they couldn't find my dad. A search ensued, and the police found his body at a nearby lake, where he had held a .38 revolver to his temple and pulled the trigger.

What hurt most about the news was the realization that I hadn't said "I love you" back to my father. That started eating at me. I felt tremendous guilt, so to get rid of that feeling, I did more drugs, had more sex, and self-medicated myself whenever I could.

At school, if anyone said something I didn't like, I put him in a hospital. One time I was hanging with my posse when we heard some kids talking trash about our gang. We hopped in our cars and went to an apartment complex where the other gang members were throwing a party. We jumped everyone except for the girls. Things got out of hand, and the cops were called.

Before we could ditch the place, the cops pulled up. I was caught and thrown in JDC—Juvenile Detention Center—where they held me for the maximum of twenty-one days. Then the authorities told me that I would be sentenced to County Jail for three years, or until I was nineteen. Apparently, the judge had heard about my gang background.

Mom hired the best defense lawyer in Orlando, some guy who cost her $5,000. He was good enough to get me off with probation, but I had to get into some type of program. Someone told Mom about House of Hope. After I arrived, I told anyone who would listen that I would talk my way out of here.

I would serve my time at House of Hope and get out. I kept to myself because none of these kids had seen what I had seen or done what I'd done. I had seen my gang friends die in fights. I had a girlfriend who aborted our unborn child. I had been there when a friend wrapped a car around the tree and died. I had lost a father to a self-inflicted gunshot wound.

One morning, I was sitting in the chapel listening to Pastor Frank. At first, I didn't want to listen, but he was from the Bronx and a former gang member himself. He seemed to know what my life had been like. I began listening more, and while we were singing worship songs, I suddenly understood the words. I understood how Christ died for *me* so that I would not perish but have eternal life with Him. I accepted Christ and became a Christian.

As I began turning my life around, I went home on a weekend pass. I ran into some of my old gang friends, but one pulled a gun on me. "Is it true you're leaving the gang?" he demanded.

"Are you kidding? I'm not leaving," I replied with my palms outstretched. I knew that if I said I was leaving the Crips, then I'd get killed. I talked my way out of a bullet to the head that night.

These days, I know I can never go to my old home again. Mom has moved several hundred miles from Orlando, and I'll go live with her when I leave House of Hope. I don't want to get killed.

I'm not sure what my future holds, but I do know that God turned my life around and took me away from the gangs. Don't try to get your friends to fill the hole in your heart. If you don't have an earthly father, you can ask God to be your father, and He will be there for you.

As for the situation with my dad, Jesus has taken away all the guilt. It was my dad's decision to do what he did, and I couldn't help it. Knowing that has really healed my heart.

Someday I hope to be a pastor. Instead of taking out people with my fists, I want to bring people into the Kingdom of God.

If we confess our sins, he is faithful and just and will forgive us our sins and purify us from all unrighteousness.

—1 John 1:9, NIV

one step too far

rose, fourteen

When I was twelve years old, I met a sixteen-year-old guy who swept me off my feet. All summer long, he treated me nice, brought me flowers and then he took me out to movies. On my birthday, he presented me with five dozen roses. He definitely wooed me, and when we kissed, our love felt so special. He said, "I love you, and I will love you forever," and I pledged my love to him.

I could tell that he wanted to do more than just kiss, but I told him I wasn't ready to go further. A few weeks passed, and I was starting the sixth grade, but I skipped the first day of school to spend the day with him. We went to his house. Both parents were off to work.

He said that since we loved each other, we should show each other how strong our love was for each other by . . . by . . . going all the way. He continued to kiss me. I said okay, let's go further. I said this because I loved him, and he loved me.

After we were done, he started laughing at me.

I didn't expect that reaction. "Why are you laughing?" I asked.

"I can't believe you're so stupid," he chuckled. "I took your virginity, and all I wanted was sex."

I felt so horrible—so used and worth about ten cents. I knew that I had just done the stupidest thing ever. I never heard from him again.

I didn't tell anyone. I *couldn't* tell anyone. I was raised in a Christian home, but I wasn't taught a lot about premarital sex. My view of myself really went down. I let myself go. I started drinking alcohol and doing drugs because I had no reason to live anymore. I had lost what was mine. I really felt sad for myself.

Word got around, though, and a lot of older guys started hitting on me. Perhaps it's because I had matured early and looked older than I really was. By the time I was thirteen, I was dating several seventeen-year-olds. I figured that since I had my virginity stolen from me, why not keep going? I slept with whomever, usually for a week before I moved on to the next guy. I slept with probably a dozen different guys.

I worried about getting pregnant. When I didn't get my period, I asked my parents to take me to a doctor. When they asked me why, I said, "Because I think I'm pregnant." They were shocked and disappointed that I had started having sex early, but they were fairly loving about it.

I decided to date someone more my own age. I met this guy in my eighth grade class. We hung out with each other for a couple of months. He had never had sex before. One time, when we were making out, he said, "Do you want to go further?"

It didn't take us long to go further. We had sex every day for a week, but then I broke it off because that's all he wanted to do. His response was to spread rumors about me, telling kids at school that I was pregnant with his kid, that I was a "ho," and that I was fat. I had gained a little weight, so to prove to everybody that I wasn't pregnant or overweight, I started exercising and stopped eating.

I got really thin. I now weighed 110 pounds on my five-foot, eight-inch frame, down thirty pounds. I looked really good. I had a problem with food, though. I started throwing up whenever I ate, and the only thing I could keep down was a Nutrigrain bar.

I became so thin that it was disgusting, so I decided to start cutting my wrists with a kitchen knife. A teacher saw my scars. He called my parents, who made me see a psychologist. I hated it. After one visit, I told my parents that if they made me go back, I would run away.

I stopped cutting my wrists, but I started hanging with an older crowd again, and we drank and did drugs. I dated another guy who was seventeen, but I told him that we weren't going to have sex, that I was fed up with the whole scene, and if that is all he wanted me for, then I'm sorry. So he dumped me. I felt rejected again.

Meanwhile, I got arrested at school when the authorities found a pint of Bacardi in my locker. I liked to sip between classes, but when I was busted, the cops came and arrested me.

Dad came and picked me up, and I was given a court date. I told Dad I didn't want to go to court, so he kept pushing the date further and further back. Finally, the court announced that my case would be heard March 16.

I really dreaded this court date. It really brought me down. I didn't want to go to jail or some program. The pressure was building on my parents as well. We argued constantly, especially over my punishment.

One afternoon, Dad told me to go rake up the leaves. Another punishment. I walked into the garage to get a rake and a garbage bag. I spotted a rope in the corner.

A rope.

I could end it all.

Life was so lousy. It certainly hadn't been much fun.

I used a six-foot stepladder to throw the rope over the rafter, which I secured with a good yank. Next, I put the rope around my neck, tightened it, and before I could think twice, I stepped off the ladder.

As soon as there was nothing under my feet, however, I realized that this was something I did not want to do. I tried to swing back onto the ladder as my hands grasped at the rope. But I didn't panic. I thought, *You know what? You thought you were going to do this, so why not?* At the same time, I couldn't believe how stupid I had been to put a rope around my neck and step off the ladder.

I fought the rope and kept trying to get a toehold on the stepladder . . . but my world was slowing down . . . and then it went black. I became unconscious.

I don't remember what happened after that, but I'm told that my father happened to come out to the garage to check on how my chores were going when he received the shock of his life. I was slowly swinging from side to side, quiet and still.

He used the stepladder to drape me over his shoulder while he untied the rope. When he set me on the ground, he thought I was dead.

He immediately ran to the kitchen to call 911. Paramedics detected a faint pulse and rushed me to the hospital.

I woke up two days later only to see the concerned look of my mother. "What happened to me, Mom?" I asked.

"You had an accident," she soothed. She could see the rope burn around me neck, but I couldn't.

I survived, and I was told that I was very lucky because most people who hang themselves die instantly when their bladder explodes. I had popped a blood vessel in my eye, which bothered me, and I noticed a numbness on my left side from my ear to my cheek and across my shoulder.

I stayed in the hospital for five days before I was transferred to a psyche ward for children. When I was released three days later, my parents brought me to House of Hope.

On my first day, I met with the girls and Miss Sara, and after they heard me share my story, they prayed for me and really cared for me. I felt this relief, so much relief, that everything would be all right.

A week or two later, though, we visited a church

that had a second-story balcony. I was standing there, looking out over the parking lot, when this overwhelming urge came over me to jump off and finish what I had started. One of the house staff, Miss Tammy, got a feeling that something might happen. She came over and pulled me away from the railing, and she brought me down to the first floor.

Inside the church, I felt this touch—I don't know what it was—but something touched me inside, and it felt like all these bad feelings were leaving me. I began praying to God, "Give me more." I opened myself up to receive His forgiveness for everything I had done, and I asked for healing of all the scars on my body. The experience touched me so much that I felt as though I was clean and a virgin again.

God has given my purity back to me, and this time around, no one will steal it and laugh in my face. While I was going through all the hurts and disappointments, I could identify with these verses from Psalm 13:

> *How long, O Lord ? Will you forget me forever? How long will you hide your face from me? How long must I wrestle with my thoughts and every day have sorrow in my heart? How long will my enemy triumph over me?*
>
> *Look on me and answer, O Lord my God. Give light to my eyes, or I will sleep in death; my enemy will say, "I have overcome him," and my foes will rejoice when I fall.*
>
> *But I trust in your unfailing love; my heart rejoices in your salvation. I will sing to the Lord, for he has been good to me.*

Now I am the one rejoicing because God spared my life and showed me His unfailing love. I know God has a special plan for my life, and I'm excited to have Him show me day by day. The Lord now orders my steps.

Lord, who may dwell in your sanctuary? Who may live on your holy hill?

—Psalms 15:1, NIV

no more labels

mike, fourteen

My dad is Arabic—his ancestors are Arab Muslims from Lebanon. He grew up Muslim, but he didn't kneel down on a prayer rug and pray five times a day or fast during Ramadan like most Islam believers. Nonetheless, he didn't eat ham or other pork products, and he still doesn't to this day.

My mom grew up as an Italian Catholic, so you can see how they had a mixed marriage. Then my mom converted my dad to Christianity, so I've been raised in the church all my life. I always had to go to church on Sunday morning. Even from a young age, though, I dealt with much depression. That's because doctors said I was born with ADHD—Attention Deficit Hyperactivity Disorder. They put me on Ritalin and Adderall when I was three years old (and I've been taking it ever since). If I didn't take my medicine and chewed on a piece of gum, for instance, I would go nuts. A little bit of sugar, and I bounced off the walls. Bottom line: I grew up medicated.

Around the age of twelve, I started realizing what else was out there. Mom, who sensed these changes in me, pulled me out of school and started homeschooling me. I didn't have any friends when I was schooled at home, and my relationship with my sister Stephanie, who was three years older, was terrible. We fought a lot and argued.

I would always hear my dad say do this, do that, and you need to do this right now, and I remember what the Bible said about obeying your father and mother, so I did what I was told to do. But I always resented the way he raised his voice and the way he spoke to me, which was usually in a yelling manner. He liked to push me up against a wall or slap me in the face with his open hand. Deep down I wanted to hit him back, but I remembered what God's Word said.

The way he treated me made me feel even more depressed, so I would walk around my neighborhood or sit in my room and listen to music. When my mom noticed how glum I was, she put me on an anti-depressant called Wellbutrin, which I had to take along with my ADHD medicines.

One night, Dad was going at me as usual, so I fought back the only way I knew how: "If you touch me again, I'm going to kill myself," I said.

"What?" he asked.

"You know you heard me. I have this pill that can kill me in three minutes." I didn't really have such a pill, but I wanted to scare him.

He called my sister to the room, and said, "Watch him for a minute." Then he told Mom what had happened. The next thing I knew, Mom drove me to the hospital, where we had to wait until four in the morning for a room in the psych ward to open up. The only good thing was that they didn't put me in a straightjacket and a padded cell. Instead, I was placed in a watch room, where people watched me from behind a mirror.

I liked the psych ward because they didn't yell or scream at me. They let me out after five days of observation and put me on a higher dose of Wellbutrin. Not long after I arrived home, my parents left Stephanie and me home alone for the weekend. They were doing that a lot because my dad won trips for being a top salesman in his company. Stephanie told me that she would have a few friends over for a little party. I said that's cool.

"You won't tell Mom and Dad will you?" she asked.

"No, you just have to give me some."

The party started mellow. My sister and her friends were drinking beers on the back porch, and her friends were getting really messed up. I got messed up, too, and after that party, I got into drugs. I knew what God's Word said, but I would do what I wanted.

The stuff cost money though. One time, Mom drove me up to an ATM and handed me her card and told me her PIN number so I could get her some cash. It was easy to get her ATM card whenever she went out of town. I went to a nearby 7-11, stuck the card in an ATM machine, typed in $260, and collected thirteen Andrew Jacksons.

My friend and I got some drugs that I thought

were good, but they really messed us up. I promised myself that I would never do that again.

A week later, I took out another $250. Again, I told myself this would be my last time. We bought some hash—that's like 100 percent THC, pure weed, straight up, one of the best types of weeds.

The next time, I took $500 out the ATM machine, which was linked to my parents' savings account. That's why my parents weren't on to me. The money was coming out of savings, not their checking account.

I stole because drugs hooked me. I went out with my friend one time and got really drugged up, but my friend had a reaction to it and almost died. That's when his parents called my parents. Mom and Dad went through my room and found some weed, pipes, drug paraphernalia, and a wad of cash. Dad called my school, and before I knew it, I was meeting with them and the counselor. I was pretty much shocked that they found out, and my parents were shocked this could happen. Mom always thought I was a good Christian boy. Now she thought of me as a liar.

My parents had heard about House of Hope, and as soon as there was an opening, they brought me here. I was mad that I had to leave home. I had gotten saved when I was a little kid, but it didn't mean anything to me. My salvation finally meant something to me during a House of Hope chapel service one morning. As I cried out to God, I felt as though I received a warm hug in return on December 10, 2002. I put down all the drugs after that. Now I can talk to my dad without arguing. I have a better understanding of him now. I learned that he yelled at me because his dad always yelled at him when he was growing up.

The Lord is teaching me who I am in Christ. I know that someone put the label on me that I was ADHD . . . I refuse to believe that curse. I know I am a child of God, and I have the potential to be the youth pastor I want to be.

If you have been labeled like I was, don't go for it. What the devil meant for destruction, God is using for good in my life. He will turn your life around, too!

But the fruit of the Spirit is love, joy, peace, patience, kindness, goodness, faithfulness, gentleness and self-control. Against such things there is no law.

—Galatians 5:22-23, NIV

when everything is a fight

jessie, fifteen

I wasn't a planned child, that's for sure. My parents met in college, started going out, and then my mother got pregnant. I guess Mom didn't believe in abortion because she kept me, and she and my father did the right thing by getting married one month before I was born. Within a year, Mom saw the real side of my father—an abusive guy who enjoyed smacking her around and saying mean things. She took me and left him, which caused a big legal fight. They fought in the courts for custody, but the judge surprised everybody when he granted full legal custody to my father. The judge made the ruling because Dad's mother was going to look after me during the day, while Mom would have continued to place me in child care since she was a full-time working mom.

It turned out that I saw Dad only on weekends because he worked in another town while Grandmother watched and raised me. He was also distracted by a series of girlfriends who would stick around until Dad started hitting them. When I turned seven or eight, I guess he thought I was old enough to get the smack treatment—physical and emotional.

"You were a mistake. If it had been up to me, you would have never been born."

Whack.

"I wish I had never met your mom at that stinking college. Then none of this would have happened."

Whack.

"You're worthless."

Whack.

If I didn't answer him fast enough, he would slam me up against a wall. If he didn't like my answer, he would slam me up against a wall. If he didn't like my tone of voice, he would slam me up against the wall. You get the picture.

He liked to start his day by slapping me in the face on the drive over to school, which would leave me in tears. I always kept my head down and tried not to make eye contact with my friends as I made my way to class. He slapped me with an open hand so there were no telltale bruises.

Just before my freshman year, I decided to leave my dad and go live with Mom, who had remarried and was living in another town. I was scared what would happen when I told him that I wasn't going to live with him anymore, but he surprised me by taking it pretty good.

I started high school by joining the marching band, where I met Charlie. He was a junior who made me feel like I was wanted. Mom had just had a baby, so she was in a mother mode and not paying much attention to me. Besides, there was a fourteen-year age gap between my stepsister and me.

Charlie never pressured me into doing drugs, but I wanted to smoke marijuana and see what everyone was talking about. I hated it, though. After smoking the first time, I gave Charlie the option—the weed or me. He said I was more important than drugs, and that is what I wanted to hear.

Charlie and I really started getting along well, so well that we lost our virginity to each other. Then we started smoking weed again. Then Charlie and I started getting into fights. His family had been abusive to him, so we were like two peas in a pod. I remember slamming him up against a washing machine and choking him. We nearly tumbled into the dryer as we fought each other.

We did a lot of kissing and making up. We started out by having protected sex, but after a while, we just went for it without a condom. We started doing it in public places for the thrill of seeing how close we could get to being caught. We had sex in dressing rooms at Dillard's and JC Penny's, in outdoor parks and cars—crazy.

Since we were engaging in risky behavior, it shouldn't have surprised me that I got pregnant, but looking back, I know it happened on the last day of school—the day I graduated from ninth grade.

Anyway, a few weeks into summer vacation, I was feeling out of sorts and snapping at Charlie. I also felt sick each morning, but I couldn't put two and two together.

"Jessie, you're pregnant" he said. "I know it."

"No, I'm not. You're crazy."

"Listen, I can see it in your face. Your body is changing, and you look different. I'm telling you that you're pregnant."

I stayed in denial. Two weeks later, Charlie said, "I'm buying you a pregnancy test."

We were at his house when we received the positive result, and we both cried all day. We were way too immature to be facing what we were facing. That night, we smoked and drank until I passed out.

I went home the next day to see Mom, who was five months pregnant herself. I found her in bed, and I cuddled up next to her.

"Mom, I have to tell you something, but I don't know how to tell you."

"Just tell me."

"I don't know how."

"Jessie, we've always been able to talk."

"But Mom, I'm so ashamed."

"Jessie, just tell me. You can do it."

"Mom, I'm pregnant."

"Excuse me?" Mom thought she didn't hear right.

"I'm pregnant."

"Are you sure?"

"I'm positive."

"I thought you were supposed to be taking your pills."

"I was. But I hadn't started them yet."

"Then leave me alone. Get out of here. You make me sick."

That hurt. I went into my room and called Charlie. "Can you come pick me up?" I asked. "My mom won't even talk to me."

Eventually, Mom came around and talked to me—about getting an abortion. She reminded me that I was just fourteen years old, a ninth grader who lacked the means to support or raise a child.

Mom made an appointment for me to see a gynecologist. I had become very sick a few weeks *before* getting pregnant, and there was concern that one of the viruses that had attacked me would affect my baby.

"Listen," said my gynecologist, a woman. "You could have a deformed baby growing in you right now. I'm talking brain damage, no arms, one arm, not the right internal organs—deformed. That's why I strongly suggest that you consider having an abortion."

I thought abortion was wrong. I didn't go to church or anything, but deep down, I thought that abortion kills someone who could be something some day.

I cried for days on end. I didn't know what to do, but with Charlie, Mom, and my aunt and uncle all saying that I was too young to have a child, that my child would be handicapped the rest of his or her life, I had to have an abortion.

I knew I wasn't strong enough to raise a mentally ill or deformed child—or give up my child up for adoption. So we decided to do it, and a date was set.

Charlie said he would pay for the abortion. He accompanied me and Mom to the clinic. I was led back to the counselor's office, where they gave me a bunch of papers to fill out. Tears ran down my face as I read and signed each consent form.

In the procedure room, they did a sonogram, which showed a living thing inside of me. I couldn't take it. I started bawling, but they told me if I continued to cry, they couldn't get it done. So I had to bottle up all my hurt and grit my teeth while it felt like a knife probing inside of me. As soon as it was over, I regretted what I had done. I felt shock. I couldn't believe I had killed my baby. I couldn't believe that I was so stupid to have unprotected sex and get pregnant.

The rest of my summer was awful. Charlie didn't hang around with me any more. Mom and I started fighting more than ever, so I decided I would show her: I began staying up all night partying. I made the mistake of believing that nothing could hold me back now. I started doing coke and taking ecstasy. I was either drinking, tripping, or walking around with a glow stick in my hand.

Early in my sophomore year, Mom and I got into a big fight when I came home one morning at eight o'clock. We started tussling, and when she slammed me into my bedroom door, I grabbed her and bit her, leaving a mark.

Mom called the police and pressed charges. When we went to court, she told the judge that she didn't want me. The judge ordered me to House of Hope.

I had so many issues to deal with . . . the hurts from my father, the rejection from my boyfriend and my mother . . . and to top that off, I had to start dealing with the hurts and trauma involved in the death of my child through the abortion. I learned about Jesus. I got saved a month or two after I began staying at House of Hope; I experienced this miraculous healing within my hurting soul. I began to understand why I yelled at people. Now if someone makes me mad, I have learned to forgive and pray for that person.

I know that my healing is a process. I am excited to have already experienced the healing love of Jesus in so many areas of my life, which is why I can't wait to see what God has for me in the future. I know He will reveal it to me as I seek His perfect will.

This year, I'm traveling with Miss Sara, speaking at Women of Faith conferences. God is using me to give hope to mothers and teenagers through my testimony. I tell others how I was like the woman at the well who was seeking for things that did not satisfy. Jesus has taught me to draw from His well, which never runs dry.

A man's wisdom gives him patience; it is to his glory to overlook an offense.

—Proverbs 19:11, NIV

plans to give you hope

elizabeth, thirty

I was abandoned as a baby and given up for adoption. After bouncing through several foster homes. I was finally adopted at the age of three—the second of five children adopted by my parents.

We were all considered special needs children. I was an ADHD kid, even though they didn't have a name for it back then. I was just known as a hyperactive child, as someone hard to handle.

Soon after I was adopted, my father would come into my room late at night and touch me where he shouldn't have. It was never rape, but it was more of a fondling thing. Although I can't remember what happened too well, his actions had a serious impact on me. For many years, I could not relate well to men in terms of relationships, and this was something that I carried with me into my teenage and adult years.

My father did this to me although he and Mom

were the first people to introduce me to Christ. The sexual abuse ended when I was sent to a Christian boarding school, at the age of eleven, because my parents were having a hard time with me. I wasn't smoking, drinking, or doing drugs, but I was still rebellious and just plain hard to deal with.

I lived at the boarding school for three years and coped with a harsh environment. When I came home, my parents were just as strict. I wasn't allowed to make phone calls or accept phone calls. I couldn't go to the movies. I couldn't do anything. About the only thing I could do was go to the backyard. That was it. Then Mom got very sick and became bedridden for some time, so all the physical housework fell on my shoulders. I also took care of my siblings, including a child with mental disabilities. That was hard, especially for someone fifteen years old.

One day, Mom was hitting my brother with a switch for some minor offense. I pleaded with her to stop, but she told me to leave the house—immediately! So I did. I walked down the street to the Sunoco gas station and slept out back for a night. I had no money in my pocket; the only thing I ate was the hot dog the attendant gave me.

The next morning, I walked over to a Little Caesar's pizza restaurant, where I was working part-time. That's where the police picked me up. They gave me a ride home, but then my parents informed me that I wouldn't be living there any longer. My new home would be House of Hope, they said. I was glad. I can honestly say that I was one of the rare ones who *wanted* to come here. I couldn't wait to leave home.

House of Hope was all girls back then. I loved the loving environment provided by Miss Sara and the house staff. I just grew as a person. You see, I already knew the Lord. I had accepted Christ when I was eleven years old on August 8, 1984. But when I arrived at House of Hope, I began soaking up God's love like a sponge. Just the difference between my home life and how House of Hope met my needs emotionally, physically, and spiritually helped me so much. I got the counseling I needed, and that's where it all came out, the sexual abuse. When that happened, there was a long period of time where my parents and I did not speak to each other, five or six years. Mom did not believe me, and my father never acknowledged his role in my abuse.

I didn't expect Dad to confess what he did, and Mom made it very difficult for us to have a relationship. I have a very forgiving heart, and that comes from the Lord. I forgave her and my father for what they did. I'm glad I did because my mom died suddenly this year at the age of sixty from unexpected heart problems. I'm thankful that God gave us back the time we had missed.

I've been married six years to my second husband, and we have four children. (One is a daughter from a previous marriage.) I sing in the choir at our church, and my husband and I enjoy running marathons. I talk to my father on the phone several times a week. We have a relationship that works.

When I turned sixteen, House of Hope helped me find my birthmother and two birthsisters. Mom had given us up in a town about eight hours from

Orlando. She could not afford to keep us, so she put us in a home to be adopted. When we found my mom, believe it or not, she was working across the street from House of Hope at a nursing home. Our reunion took place in the reception office. The tears flowed as we all rejoiced.

I still have a relationship with my birthmother and my birthsisters and stay in phone contact. You know, they are totally different from me, and I'm the only Christian in the bunch. I pray that I can be a ray of light to them and lead them to Christ.

I pray every day that my birthmom will become a Christian. She's getting up in age, and anything could happen. I want to see her in heaven. The same goes for my sisters, and I think the Lord will grant those prayers. In fact, I know He will.

And here's my advice to young people reading my story: Always rely on the Lord. Don't forget that prayer works. Things may not work out the way you want them to, but things will work eventually in God's way and God's own timing. His hand is always on us, carrying us through what we may think is the worst time of our lives, but He is still there. I think back to that time when I spent the night alone at the Sunoco station. The Lord had His hand on me back then, and He still does today.

Looking back through the years, I can see much better how God has a purpose for me. I keep that in mind today when I'm going through something that seems difficult. Believe me, that helps.

The Bible verse that has been meaningful to me is: "For I know the plans I have for you," declares the Lord, "plans to prosper you and not to harm you, plans to give you hope and a future" (Jeremiah 29:11, NIV). No matter what you've been through, God wants to prosper you and give you hope and a future, too.

❦

He lifted me out of the slimy pit, out of the mud and mire; he set my feet on a rock and gave me a firm place to stand.

—Psalm 40:2, NIV

a stolen childhood

nina, fourteen

When I was just a few months old, my father walked out on my mother, and to this day, I have not heard from him, nor do I know where he lives. My mom tells me that I was an early walker as a baby. Unfortunately, at nine months of age, I walked myself into our backyard pool when nobody was around. Two minutes later, my frantic mother discovered my nearly lifeless body lying at the bottom of the pool. She dove in and brought me to the surface.

My skin was all shades of purple and blue as paramedics rushed me to the hospital in a heroic attempt to save my life. After being stabilized, I remained in a coma for one week before I opened my eyes and began moving again. Doctors did not give my mother much hope for the future; they said I would likely be a vegetable for the rest of my life.

I not only survived, but I soon thrived. Mom and my two older brothers took good care of me. We lived in Orlando, and Mom dated a lot and was friendly with many people, including a lonely grandfatherly type we called "Pop." My mom always invited him to go to church with us.

Pop was a child molester. He began touching my private parts in inappropriate ways when I was three years old, and this continued for years. Mom, meanwhile, got married for the third time, and I liked my new stepdad. He was always sweet and took me places, but the marriage didn't last long because he would lie and steal money from her.

We had a dysfunctional family, that's for sure. When I was in first grade, my twelve-year-old brother visited family in the New York City area and never came back. This custody issue really upset Mom. I guess there wasn't anything she could do about it.

When I was eight years old, this Pop did more than fondle me, which he usually did two or three times a week as I was growing up. On this occasion, he dragged me into the laundry room. I guess Mom was off doing something else, but he hit me a couple of times and then covered my mouth with his hand. He said it would be better if I didn't say anything. I cried a lot and didn't know what was happening, so I stopped trying to resist. Then he raped me, and when he was done, he threatened to hurt my mom if I breathed a word of this to anybody.

Not long after that, Mom invited Pop to go to church with us, where she was involved in the youth program. During the church service, I told Mom that I needed to go to the bathroom, so she asked Pop if he'd walk me to the restrooms. That's when Pop marched me into the boy's bathroom and raped me again! No one walked in because it was right in the middle of the pastor's sermon.

My nightmare ended when I was ten years old. Pop, who was getting up there in years, began experiencing failing health. He entered a nursing home, where I later heard that he tried to go after the nurses, but he died shortly after. I breathed a huge sigh of relief.

I had been attending a Christian academy, but Mom moved me over to the local public school when I was in third grade. I lied and stole a lot. For instance, I stole a turtle from the library because I wanted it so bad and we had no money. Third grade was also the year that Mom started dating a guy named Rick. One afternoon, Mom picked me up from school and casually informed me that she and Rick were married that morning before the justice of the peace. I didn't even know that they were going to get married. That was number four for her.

At first, I thought the marriage was cool. He had four kids, including three sons and one daughter, and I looked forward to having some siblings in the house. Mom now had the money to put me back into the private Christian academy again, so I returned for the fourth grade. But Rick became the most physically abusive guy to my mom, always cussing her out and acting like a madman.

One evening as he was putting me to bed, I didn't want to say my goodnight prayers. I had an attitude, so he beat me with his muscular hands until the whole right side of my face was black and blue. The next day, Mom told me to lie and say that I had been hit by a soccer ball. The school administrators didn't believe my story, so they called Social Services, who made an investigation. They gave Rick a warning and told him not to strike me again.

Peace reigned for a while, but the usual cuss-outs and fighting and arguing soon reared their heads again. Mom kicked Rick out of the house at least twice. She hated his kids because they were sexually active and doing drugs, and she didn't want that in the house. Rick moved back in for the third time and tried to make it work.

When I was in seventh grade, I met some older guys in my youth group who were gang members. They came to the youth group for the free pizza and basketball games. These were sixteen-, seventeen-year-old guys, and I started going out with Jamal, the gang leader. He told me I could be in the gang, too, but he wouldn't tell me which one it was. "You have to get initiated in it first," he said, so I asked him where I could sign up. He gave me a lot of free drugs: ecstasy, pot, and angel dust.

Jamal had to travel a lot as a gang member, and it seemed as though he was always going to North Carolina for something. Then, in the middle of seventh grade, I learned that my twenty-year-old brother Alex was found dead on the front porch of his frat house. Someone had spiked his drink with an overdose amount of GHB. We flew to New York City for the funeral, which was ghastly because it was an open-casket service.

Our return flight was scheduled to leave at 10 p.m. on Monday, September 10, 2001, out of JFK Airport. Our flight was delayed. At first, the gate staff said we would be leaving at midnight. Then

2 a.m. Then 4 a.m. After spending all night at the airport, we finally boarded our plane at dawn and took off at 7 a.m., the same time that Todd Beamer and others were checking in for United Flight 93 in nearby Newark.

We landed in Orlando around 9:30 in the morning to the most surreal scene. Everyone was acting frantically at the airport, and we soon learned why. Two passenger planes had crashed into the World Trade Center. We had just been there!

About a month after 9/11, I started getting into more drugs, started skipping school, and I started sneaking out with older guys. It didn't help matters when the cops picked me up at 5 a.m. as I was walking home after an evening of fun.

My parents yelled at me, and I reacted violently. I threw beer bottles and threatened to kill them. I kicked Mom and punched her. I was stressed because one of Rick's sons—a half-brother who was the same age as me—kept trying to force himself on me. Twice he tried to rape me, and I had to fight him off. I knew how to handle myself since I hung out with a gang. I was devastated, though, when I heard that Jamal had been killed in a gunfight. I didn't believe the news until I read it in the newspaper.

All this whacked-out stuff and behavior turned me suicidal. I was on Prozac for depression, so one time I gulped 150 tablets in front of Mom. Another time, I took twenty-five Tylenol PMs just before I went to bed; I woke up the next morning throwing up all over the place.

Mom noticed a bunch of knives missing from the kitchen. She found seven butcher knives under my pillow. Mom confronted me, but she knew that I was a ticking time bomb, an eighth-grader with a pierced belly button who was stealing lunches at school and involved in all sorts of destructive behavior.

A few weeks into my eighth-grade year I entered House of Hope. I had been raised in a so-called Christian home, but I didn't know Christ. I had never accepted the relationship—I had Him in my head, but not in my heart.

As I went through counseling, I learned that I had to forgive my father for abandoning me. I had to forgive my mother for marrying many times. Through special prayers and counseling, I overcame my sense of loss for the terrible sexual abuse that I had encountered.

Pastor Frank was awesome with me. When he talked about how he screwed up when he was young but Christ still opened His arms to him, that touched me. I needed to give Christ my whole heart. Only He could take away my deep pain, my feelings of abandonment, and my anger for having lost a childhood. Nonetheless, I should have died many times, starting with the day that I walked into a backyard pool when nobody was looking. Now I know that God has a purpose for my life, and I want to fulfill that purpose.

When I accepted Christ back into my life, I prayed that He would come in and renew my family and renew my heart and start working with my life. He has been faithful to that request, and now I have a really good relationship with my mom.

Christ has kept me here on this earth for some reason, and I'm going to stick around and find out why. When I came to House of Hope, I was full of hurts. The Scripture that is special to me is found in Matthew 11:28-30 (NIV): "Come to me, all you who are weary and burdened, and I will give you rest. Take my yoke upon you and learn from me, for I am gentle and humble in heart, and you will find rest for your souls. For my yoke is easy and my burden is light."

If you are reading this today and you have some hurts, I want to encourage you to go to someone or some program for help. Maybe you think programs are stupid. Let me tell you that I felt that way, too, but I was wrong. House of Hope saved my life. Now I know that I have a destiny, and I will fulfill it with God's help.

Give ear to my words, O Lord, consider my sighing.

—Psalms 5:1, NIV

the pleasant side effects

thomas, sixteen

I was adopted at birth by the only parents I've ever known. Dad and Mom raised me in a Christian home, and they later had two children of their own after I arrived on the scene.

I was a little monster when I started school. After acting up, my parents sent me to see a battery of psychologists, who diagnosed me with ADD—Attention Deficit Disorder. I began taking Ritalin in kindergarten, which made me more hyper and crazy in the classroom. I ran around, picked up chairs and threw them, and bullied classmates on the playground. In the first grade, I got a referral for throwing a kid into a fence and mashing his face against it.

Later I calmed down some, but I never could do my classwork. I still got good grades though because I'm pretty smart and because I wanted to play football and wrestle. Still, school and me weren't a good mix. Mom tried to homeschool me during sixth grade, but that didn't go well, so that summer she and Dad sent me to a program in Colorado called the Attachment Center. I hated that place. I was dealing with issues I didn't have—like attachment disorders. They said I hadn't bonded with my parents, but they were missing the problem. They didn't know that I was bipolar and a manic-depressive.

What does that mean? It's like you are really depressed and you don't want to get out of bed. The manic component means that you are so wired that you do crazy stuff and can't sleep for two days. When my parents went to bed, I would hop out my window and go and see my friends. The depressive component means just that—you get really down.

The Attachment Center insisted that I go on drugs—medications like Prozac, Wellbutrin, and Risperdal. One of the side effects, unfortunately, is weight gain. I ballooned up to 240 pounds—a gain of ninety pounds. I was fortunate that I never got teased in middle school, though. My friends saw me as a big kid with big bones.

I started doing stupid stuff when I returned to public school in eighth grade. I rode my bike around with guys and spray-painted buildings, broke windows, and pulled sinks off the walls. Two weeks before the end of school, some kid looked at me funny, so I pushed him up against a wall, kicked him, and broke his arm. That got me expelled.

After I got kicked out, I started smoking weed with my friends. Through that summer, I progressively got worst. I went to concerts and parties and drank and did drugs. I abused my prescription drugs and used heroin and peyote.

I was tight with my dealer, so I sold for him and paid for my drugs that way. My parents never knew, or my friends. I didn't want them to narc me and turn me in.

In ninth grade, I returned to school, but I got arrested twice—once for dealing and the other time public intoxication, alcohol use, and indecent exposure. What happened is that I was drunk and some friends pantsed me in the schoolyard.

That arrest landed me in Teen Drug Court and eventually House of Hope. A month after I arrived, we had a "Week to Seek" with Pastor Frank. We had a bunch of chapel services—one every day and every night. The power of God's truth had sunk into me. I knew I needed God, and I knew I wouldn't be able to live without him. I was saved a little more than a month later.

I don't think about drugs any more. My relationship with my family is much better. I'm not scared that someone will pick me up and take me off to jail. I don't have to look over my shoulder now.

These days, I read the Word as much as I can. I've highlighted the following verses in my Bible that are special to me:

- "Do not envy violent people; don't copy their ways. Such wicked people are an abomination to the LORD, but he offers his friendship to the godly" (Proverbs 3:31-32, NLT).

- "Endure suffering along with me, as a good soldier of Christ Jesus. And as Christ's soldier, do not let yourself become tied up in the affairs of this life, for then you cannot satisfy the one who has enlisted you in his army. Follow the Lord's rules for doing his work, just as an athlete either follows the rules or is disqualified and wins no prize" (2 Timothy 2:3-5, NLT).

The other thing I like to do to bolster my faith is to listen to worship CDs—albums with praise and worship songs. I pop one of those CDs in my player, and I know I'm going to stay on the straight and narrow path. If you need a faith lift, turn on some good Christian music. It will give you peace.

This is a true saying: If we die with him, we will also live with him. If we endure hardship, we will reign with him. If we deny him, he will deny us. If we are unfaithful, he remains faithful, for he cannot deny himself.

—2 Timothy 2:11-13, NLT

when trust built up

barbara, thirty-one

I grew up in South Carolina with moral parents; however, they were not Christians. Daddy, who was forty-eight years old when I was born, was an alcoholic. Although he always had health problems, it still came as a shock when he died from a stroke when I was eleven years old. I was my daddy's little girl!

My older brothers, Momma, and I never sat down and cried together—never took time to grieve his loss. A few weeks after Daddy's death, Momma was diagnosed with breast cancer, which necessitated the removal of one of her breasts and radiation treatment. Everything was a blur during those difficult days. My reaction was to rebel. I started skipping class, back talking to elders, and getting into some real catfights at school. When Momma got out of the hospital, there was nothing she could do to control me. I snuck out at night and experimented with drugs and drinking. Someone showed me how to shoot Demerol—a painkiller—into my legs with a syringe.

I overdosed at the age of twelve, and from that point on, I was in and out of the hospital, treatment programs, and secular counseling, but nothing helped me. When I was thirteen, Momma found out about House of Hope, which had only been open a few years in Orlando. One night, I could tell that something was different with Momma. At eight o'clock, she announced that we were going for a car ride—to Orlando. We arrived at 3 a.m., but the office wasn't open. Can you imagine that? I was furious with her and did not want to get out of the car.

I was not happy about coming into the program. There were only twelve girls back then, so House of Hope was much different than it is today. All I knew back then, however, was that House of Hope was much different than anything I had experienced before. I figured I would do my time and fake my way through the program.

Miss Sara was very involved with all the girls, to the point that she required us to take notes in church. Then she would critique our notes, just like the schoolteacher she was. We really got to know her, and trust was built between us. I still didn't want to become a Christian, though, and I even got mad at one of the girls who gave her life to the Lord.

I couldn't understand how God could love me. I remember talking with Miss Sara about that one time. Finally, at one point, she said, "You should read Romans 10:9-10, and there, you will find your answer."

So I looked it up and read it over and over (the

verses are printed at the end of this chapter). I really meditated on those words and what they meant. Finally, one day it all came together. I remember running into Miss Sara's office. "I got it! I got it" I screamed. Then Miss Sara sat and prayed with me, and I asked Jesus into my heart.

The Lord really changed my life, so much so that I was able to leave House of Hope eight months later and return home. Mom, unfortunately, was getting sicker and sicker, and she knew she was dying. At one point, Miss Sara asked Momma what she could do to help her. "Could you take care of my little girl?"Momma asked.

So I returned to House of Hope and helped as a "junior staff" member—a title that Sara invented for me. I helped around the grounds, painting rooms and ministering to the other girls.

Momma died in December of my senior year of high school. I was seventeen, but I stayed in South Carolina and finished my school year. After graduation, I moved back to House of Hope and became part of the house staff. I lived with the younger girls—those twelve, thirteen, and fourteen years old—and on my days off, I lived with Miss Sara and her niece Jenny until I was twenty-one years old. Working on the house staff was one of the best things I ever did. There were days I got stressed and tired, but I bonded with those girls and built a close relationship with Miss Sara.

I left my job with the House of Hope and my home with Miss Sara to marry my husband, Mark, whom I knew in high school. I thought I would cry when Miss Sara sat in the first row and was seated in place of my mother. She helped me plan my entire wedding. Walter Meloon, a House of Hope board member, gave me away. Mark was stationed in the military, and we lived in Hawaii and Montana, where Sara visited me one time. She offered me a position at House of Hope interviewing the girls and the parents before they were accepted into the program. Mark could do maintenance and work on the grounds.

We worked at House of Hope for a year, leaving only because we had a heart to go to Africa as missionaries. We worked at a Bible school in the middle of the bush in Zambia.

These days, I have a three-year-old daughter named Autumn, who has already given her life to the Lord.

As I look back, I'm thankful that Sara was really big about us memorizing Scripture, so big, in fact, that she rewarded us with a $20 bill when we memorized twenty verses. She taught us how to listen to the Lord and taught us the importance of taking time to read the Word.

Having that foundation has made such a difference in my life. I can still quote Psalm 91 in its entirety. There's something about the Word when it comes out of your spirit, and that's why memorizing Scripture is so important.

It turns out Miss Sara knew what she was talking about after all.

If you confess with your mouth, "Jesus is Lord," and believe in your heart that God raised him from the dead, you will be saved. For it is with your heart that you believe and are justified, and it is with your mouth that you confess and are saved.

—Romans 10:9-10, NIV

running a red light

rachel, sixteen

Up until I was eight years old, I grew up very normally in a very normal home. I had a mother and father who loved me and two older siblings: Lacy, who was twelve years old, and Vin, my nine-year-old brother.

One time, my Aunt Vicki was staying with us for a few days. It was dinnertime, and Dad was home sick and Mom was cooking dinner. Lacy and Vin really wanted to go roller-blading at a local rink after dinner, but I wanted to stay home and hang with Dad. My father and I were really close, and I liked being with him when he was home. Aunt Vicki volunteered to drive my older sister and brother to the roller-blading rink.

They never got there.

A drunk driver blew through a red light and struck the passenger side of my parent's Volkswagen sedan, killing Vin instantly. Lacy survived twenty-one days until a tragic episode involving a medical malpractice situation resulted in her death. The doctors accidentally gave her drugs in the wrong dosage. My Aunt Vicki was the only survivor, despite the fact that all three were wearing their seatbelts.

Everything changed after that.

Where I had been a happy kid, now I walked around the house as one lonely, depressed person. My parents were Christians, so their faith helped them get through the tragic losses, but I didn't look to God. I never wanted to do anything or have fun. How could I? If I couldn't go to the mall or go roller-blading with my sister, then I didn't want to do anything.

I lost my motivation to do well in school, so Mom pulled me out and started homeschooling me. That didn't work, so when I began high school in ninth grade, I was a poor student. My parents thought a private Christian academy would turn things around, and for a while, it did. In the tenth grade, I was a popular cheerleader who had plenty of friends, including a good boyfriend.

One night after a football game, a mutual acquaintance introduced me to a senior from the school we had just played against. His name was Donny. I guess he wanted to meet me after he saw me doing cheer during the game.

"Hey, you all want to get something to eat?" he asked the group.

We all did, and that night, we definitely had eyes for each other. He was three years older—a buff, good-looking guy who swept me off my feet. When our evening was over, he said he wanted to see me again, and I said yes. I quickly broke up with my old boyfriend.

I think I was attracted to Donny because he was the bad boy type. That sounded exciting to me. He invited me to his house for a big party where there were a ton of kids doing all sorts of drinking and drugging. Donny lived with his mom, but she didn't care.

I hadn't done anything bad up to that point, but I made up for lost time. I totally fell in with this new crowd, but I had to keep it all a secret from my parents. A few weeks later, I told my parents that I was going over to Rachel's house, when in fact I was going to Donny's to get drunk, but I couldn't reach Rachel. I went anyway. Then Rachel called my house looking for me, and my parents quickly put two-and-two together.

Mom got some directions from my friend and drove over to Donny's house. She found me standing in front of the house, totally smashed. That was also the first time she met Donny.

Mom hustled me into the car and drove me home. The next morning she said she was disappointed in my behavior, which would result in me being grounded.

I think a night or two passed until I got all dressed up and walked out of the front door without saying goodbye. I was out of control, and there was nothing my parents could do about it. After a while, I stopped attending the Christian academy and switched to Donny's high school.

I was a virgin when I met Donny, but that only lasted a month. He was eighteen, suave and sophisticated—and very sexually experienced. He got me drunk one night, and with my defenses down, there was little I could do to resist.

Then something weird happened. I got drunk on another night, and I found myself in bed with this other guy who wanted sex. I let him do it. It was just a one-night stand, but I got pregnant anyway.

I found out I was pregnant when I skipped my period and told Mom about it. She ran me down to the doctor, and a pregnancy test confirmed my condition.

My situation was unusual from many pregnant teens—my parents did not want me to have an abortion. I didn't want an abortion, and Donny didn't want me to have an abortion, even though it wasn't his child.

I stopped drinking and doing drugs because I knew that wouldn't be good for the life growing in me. I still hung out at Donny's parties, though. One evening, a guy that my boyfriend hated became belligerent with me. We were standing in front of Donny's house when this drunk animal grabbed me and threw me against a car. I landed on my stomach and felt immediate a huge stabbing pain.

All night I was in great discomfort, and when I awoke the next morning, the bleeding began. I miscarried that day, three months into my pregnancy.

I went from being bad to *really* bad. I ran away all the time. I stole money from my parents so Donny could buy drugs for us. I got into fights with girls over my boyfriend. One time I was in Dillard's department store, and I tried to buy something with Mom's Dillard's card. When the sales clerk noticed that I wasn't my mother, she tried to grab me, but I fought back, which created a scene. I was arrested and put on probation.

I constantly broke my probation, so the judge said his hands were tied. He had to send me away to a residential state program. I was there for four months, really struggling, when the most humiliating thing happened to me. Early one evening, my roommate—a female—jumped on me while I lay in bed. I screamed for help, but no one heard me. I continued to try to push her off, but she did not let up. She violated me with her hand, and I felt like I had been raped.

For two days, I sniffled and cried, but I didn't tell anyone what happened. Finally, two girls asked me why I was crying, and I told them what happened. Within the hour, cops arrived, and before I knew it, I was transferred to House of Hope.

I'm telling you that I was so hungry for a change, so hungry for God that I got saved the first week I was here. I could really relate to Pastor Frank because he seemed to have experienced exactly what I had gone through.

God has helped me more than anybody, and more than drugs and sex and guys ever will. I can depend on Him and be confident that He's not going to use me like so many others have. God just wants to love me, and I want to love Him back.

Maybe you, too, have lost someone you love, and there's a hole in your heart. I tried everything to fill that void in my life. I went through a lot of hurt when I finally realized that only God could fill that void. I want to encourage you to give Him a chance. He will show you real love.

He sent forth his word and healed them; he rescued them from the grave.

—Psalms 107:20, NIV

just scratching the surface

trever, fourteen

My parents were divorced before I was born, and I never saw my father until I was seven years old. Mom remarried when I was three or four and had two children right away, but she had gotten divorced a second time when I started first grade. We went to live at my aunt's house in Park City, Utah, a ski area in the Wasatch Mountains not far from Salt Lake City, because Mom was diagnosed with MS—multiple sclerosis.

At a very young age, I was forced to be the father to my little brother and sister. I had to wake up early and make them breakfast, get them up and dressed, comb their hair, and bathe them at night. Mom was so weak that she couldn't run a brush through their hair. She walked with a cane and thought she was going blind.

One day out of the blue, I got a phone call from my real dad. This was the first time I ever talked to this man. He said he wanted to see me because he missed me, which was weird. He didn't know who I was.

Mom drove me to a mall in Salt Lake City, where I spent the day with him. Then I didn't hear from my father for a few months, which bothered me, because I wanted to hang out with him and meet my two half-brothers. While this was going on, I still had to take care of my mom and my little brother and sister. I was forced to grow up too soon, and I think I acted twice my age.

Mom, who was a Christian, started praying and getting in the Word, and she got miraculously healed overnight. Her MS went away, and she wasn't blind anymore. That miracle took a load off my back, but the entire experience damaged me because I was forced to deal with things that little kids shouldn't have to deal with. For instance, I preferred to hang out with older kids. I was big into snowboarding, so as a fourth grader, I 'boarded with my seventh and eighth grade friends, who introduced me to smoking weed.

By the time I reached the seventh grade, I was going out with girls two, three years old than me, and I became sexually active with them. I had my girlfriends and could totally do my own thing. I still acted like a Christian around my mom, but I was totally different around my friends.

Sooner rather than later, though, I began fighting with Mom around the clock. One of the biggest things was her insistence on me reading the Bible with her. "It's time to read," she would say, but I would blow her off and say, "No, I'm going to my room." I felt that she was shoving God down my throat, and I came to hate anything that had to do with religion.

In seventh and eighth grade, we got into screaming matches. She really ticked me off when she searched around my room and found a porn magazine that a friend had lent me. She also found some of my CDs that she didn't like. She yelled at me not to listen to that trash. We began screaming at each other, and there couldn't have been an inch between our noses. We were flaming hot at each other. Then she grabbed me by the arm, twisted it, and I flipped out. I pushed her and started swinging. She scratched and clawed back. After our tussle, I ran out the door—this was the middle of winter—wearing just a T-shirt, shorts, and socks. I spent the night at a friend's house down the street.

I went to school the next day with scratches all over my neck, black and blue bruises on my chin, and a throbbing headache. Mom had pinned me up against a wall and kept slamming my head against it. Word got around school about what had happened. I received a note to see a school counselor. After interviewing me she called Social Services, who came to our house and took control of the situation. Mom and I got some counseling, and things got better for about a year. We didn't argue much and kept to ourselves.

After I started ninth grade, however, the truce was over. We got into a *huge* argument. I shoved her and ran into the kitchen, where I grabbed a steak knife. "If you don't stop, I'll kill you!" I yelled.

A look of horror came over Mom's face. I fell to the ground crying. "I'm sorry, Mom, I really am."

She called the cops anyway. They busted in, and the next thing I know, I saw a gun in my face. I'm telling you, it was crazy. I ended staying at the Juvenile Detention Center for ten days.

The judge wanted to put me in this program called Observation and Assessment for an extensive psychological evaluation. The Observation and Assessment program is a lock-up where they medicate you and watch how you respond. I was looking at three months of total isolation.

In the middle of the court proceedings, Mom asked whether she could approach the judge. She held a pamphlet from House of Hope in her hand.

"Your Honor, my aunt and uncle used to work at House of Hope as schoolteachers, and they say this would be an excellent program for my son. Would you give us permission to move to Florida instead of putting him away?"

I don't know why the judge said yes, but by the grace of God, he let us go. Just one problem: we had no money to get to Orlando. Then Mom's church donated enough money to send me there ahead of the family. I flew out in November and stayed with my aunt and uncle until a bed opened up at House of Hope a couple of months later. As soon as I was in, Mom and my siblings headed east in a U-Haul.

I knew as soon as I arrived at House of Hope that this was as good as it gets, especially compared to that Observation and Assessment program back in Utah. During my counseling sessions, some things began surfacing. I was angry toward my father for abandoning me. I was angry with Mom for getting sick and not being a mom to me. I was angry that I was robbed of my childhood.

A month or two after I came to House of Hope, we had this preacher come by who explained God's love and God's forgiveness. I broke down and started crying. This time I could feel a difference in myself. I thought I knew all that Bible stuff before. I could ace any Bible quiz, but I never acted on it.

Brian, one of the guys I met at House of Hope, really ministered to me. He was a former gang member that I could tell was close to God. His praying and praising of God showed in his life. He told me to let go all the pride and the crap that I thought I loved. He said that I had to realize what I really had, which was Jesus Christ.

That's all I have right now. As for my past, I've lost everything. I've lost my freedom. I lost the snow and the mountains of Utah. I could have been a pro snowboarder making $2,000 in photo shoots for snowboarding magazines. Here in Orlando, I've heard it doesn't snow much. I'm still looking for the mountains. In the meantime, I've found Jesus.

I know I'm in a better place, though. Whatever I've lost, God has something better waiting for me. If that means I can't snowboard again, that's okay. I have a much better life than I once had.

Trust in the Lord with all your heart and lean not on your own understanding; in all your ways acknowledge him, and he will make your paths straight.

—Proverbs 3:5-6, NIV

the hammer that breaks rocks

matthew, thirteen

I was born in Johnson City, Tennessee, but I don't know my real mom or dad because I was adopted when I was four months old. I was raised in Raleigh, North Carolina, for nine years before we moved to Orlando.

Dad was a bishop in a non-denominational church, so I was raised in a Christian home. Once we moved to Orlando, I just started having anger problems. Things bothered me. I wondered: *Why I was adopted? Why didn't my real mom want me?*

You have these questions when your parents are white and you're black. I mean, anyone could tell that I was adopted. My parents adopted a second child, but he was white.

When I was twelve, my friends introduced me to pornography. They showed me how to steal magazines with pictures of naked women from the convenience stores, and then they taught me how to find pornography on the Web sites.

My problems with pornography started small, but

they soon got bigger and bigger. I didn't know how addictive this stuff was to look at. I prayed for God to get me out of it, and that seemed to work for a while. I still got depressed a lot, though. I didn't want to talk to anybody, and whenever my friends tried to say something to me, I would hang up on them or cuss them out.

I was even depressed on my birthday on August 22, 2002. I sat there like a lump of coal at our family outings. Sometimes I would laugh and play around when I felt like it, but most of the time, I moped around. I wanted to take drugs, and there was no way for me to get drugs because I was a PK—a preacher's kid. My friends gave me some drugs, but they also showed me how I could crush up over-the-counter drugs like Motrin and Advil to get a little buzz going. I took those pills from bottles in our medicine cabinet. I used sugar pills as replacements. Motrin and Advil really didn't do anything, but it was kind of a thrill to get away with it anyway under my parents' noses.

Another six months went by, and I just went downhill. Some new kids at school showed me these Web sites for paintball guns, real guns, and airsoft rifles, which shoot pebbles and BBs.

I got right back into pornography when my friends brought it to school. They had it in their lockers, and each time they showed me a picture of a naked woman, something inside me was stirred up. I couldn't stop myself from looking. I started downloading all kinds of stuff on my computer until Dad found out. That's when he found that I had visited over 400 porn sites.

My dad and mom prayed with me about what was best for me. Dad then called Miss Sara and said the best thing I could do was to go to House of Hope and get some help. My father said it would be fun, and I would learn a lot.

My first day at House of Hope was a Monday. I sat in the front office while my parents were getting counseling from Miss Sara, and I just sat there. The people that work here said everything would be all right, but I cursed them.

I checked into the house and met my roommates, but they were all dominant because I was the new kid. I got into a lot of fights with them. After a while, I didn't want to fight anymore. At a chapel service with Pastor Frank, I rededicated my life to God. Now I can look at a girl and not lust over her. I have a better relationship with my parents, and I'm making progress in every area of my life.

I know my story sounds simple, but it's not. I have had to learn to make the right choices. When I get mad, I go up to somebody who has my best interests at heart and talk to him or her about my problems. Things always go better after I've talked about them.

These days, I feel soothed when I read the 23rd Psalm, and I hope it soothes you as well:

The Lord is my shepherd, I shall not be in want.
He makes me lie down in green pastures, he leads me beside quiet waters,
he restores my soul.
He guides me in paths of righteousness
for his name's sake.
Even though I walk through the valley of the shadow of death,
I will fear no evil,
for you are with me;

your rod and your staff
they comfort me.

You prepare a table before me
in the presence of my enemies.
You anoint my head with oil;
my cup overflows.
Surely goodness and love will follow me
all the days of my life,
and I will dwell in the house of the Lord forever.

Another Bible verse that has helped me is found in Jeremiah 23:29 (NIV): "Is not my word like fire," declares the Lord, "and like a hammer that breaks a rock in pieces?"

When I pray God's words, when I am tempted to do wrong, God's words are like a mighty hammer smashing my hardest problems to pieces. Just in case you may have been adopted, or if you have had a problem with friends who try to get you on the wrong road, or if you've had problems with pornography, trust God's Word.

The moment you have a thought about lust, quote 1 Corinthians 6:18, which says: "Flee from sexual immorality." It's an easy verse to memorize. If you change your mind, God will change your heart as He has changed mine. Your mind can be renewed by reading the Word.

The body is not meant for sexual immorality, but for the Lord.

—1 Corinthians 6:13, NIV

the toughest discipline of all

missy, fourteen

Growing up in Orlando, all I can remember is that my mother and father argued a lot and that my older sister, Martha, and I didn't get along. Perhaps that's because Martha and I came from completely different planets. I'm the sporty, tomboy sort who likes to break a sweat, while Martha was the girly-girly type into music and art.

My argumentative parents finally threw in the towel and separated when I was eight years old, and for the next few years, all I can remember is Mom going in and out of different boyfriends. Dad? He was always gone on business. They somehow managed to share joint custody. We lived with my mother during the week and then spent the weekend with Dad after he got home from yet another business trip. Even after they broke up, Mom and Dad still argued, and their number-one topic of contention was the question of custody.

One weekend, we were staying at Dad's house

when Martha and my father got into—you guessed it—an argument. Dad lost his temper and slapped her across the face. Martha was shocked, and she continually rubbed where she had been whacked. The rubbing caused the wound to look much worse, and when Martha and I returned home, Mom naturally wondered what happened.

"He beat me," Martha said, and before you could say the words "restraining order," Mom traveled to an emergency courtroom, where a judge granted her sole custody and ordered my father not to see us for three weeks. Afterward, the Orlando Police Department had to be present during all visits.

A couple of weeks passed, and I called Dad to see how he was doing. He sounded angry, but then he calmed down.

"I love you," he said.

"I love you too, Dad, but don't do anything stupid because of your anger issues."

Then I gave the phone to my sister and ran to the next room and picked up another phone so I could listen in.

Dad began yelling at Martha, saying that he hated her and my mom and that he could never forgive them.

That's when I heard the phone drop and a bunch of static.

"Dad! Dad!" my sister cried out.

Then we heard a loud bang that sounded like a gunshot! All I can remember is running to the next room, screaming for Mom, before I passed out in shock.

When I came to, Mom was out in the middle of

the street, talking with the police. I walked outside to talk to her, and when she saw me, she collapsed in a heap. While she was tended to, a social worker escorted me back to the house, where she told me that my dad had committed suicide.

Following Dad's death, I became very rebellious. I was nine years old, and Mom had to take me out of a private Catholic school and put me into a public school, where I was introduced to a whole lot of things. For the next couple of years, I started hanging out at teen clubs in Orlando, where I got into smoking and drinking.

I never wanted to come home. I preferred hanging out with my new friends, Mary Ann and her brother, Brad. They were into things like stealing cars and dealing drugs, and that seemed exciting to me. Since Brad was a friend, he didn't charge us for the marijuana and ecstasy.

As I got older, I started going to more teen bars, especially the ones where the bouncers didn't do anything about the kids doing drugs inside the club. Mary Ann and I also got into guys, and I became sexually active when I was thirteen. We would stay out at clubs until four or five o'clock in the morning, showing absolutely no respect for ourselves.

Mom, meanwhile, was flipping out. I was gone all the time, totally out of control, while my older sister was getting really rebellious. Mom found out about House of Hope, and she made us go to Tuesday night family counseling. I didn't like it when the counselors would pinpoint things I didn't like about myself—like no self-respect or respect for others. Those counseling sessions made me so mad that I would race out to the car and sulk.

My sister started acting better, which put all the attention on me. Finally, Mom had enough. After staying up all night at some club and sleeping until four o'clock in the afternoon, Mom announced that I would be making a move—to House of Hope.

I hated Mom so much for making me go here. I didn't want to be at House of Hope, so I didn't show any emotion and wanted to prove to everyone that they couldn't reach me.

Then I saw God's love for me through the people at House of Hope. As I was beginning to deal with my issues in counseling, I knew my heart was softening, but I still had rebellious thinking. After four months, I no longer had the desire to go out with my old best friends. This was not how I wanted to live.

Although my attitude changed, I was still getting into trouble for breaking the rules. Three other girls and I decided to run away from the program. Once we were back on the streets, the old pressures stared kicking in. Someone had some weed, and at first I said no, but when everyone was smoking, I said, *Why not?*

One of the girls who ran away with me has an uncle who is a local sheriff, and he had all the cops looking for us. We were found and brought back, and when I returned, my heart was softened to God. I had a big heart change, and at chapel, I gave my life to Christ. Two weeks later, Mom did the same thing! Since then, life has been very good.

What I've learned through all this is that God has a plan for you. He died for me, even though I thought my future consisted of sitting around an apartment watching TV, selling drugs, driving around in stolen cars, and making good money. At one time, I really thought I was going to do that the rest of my life.

But God knew better, and I'm glad He did. He disciplines the ones he loves, and I sure got disciplined, but I also know He loves me and wants me to be His.

He heals the brokenhearted and binds up their wounds.

—Psalm 147:3, NIV

running into a brick wall

bobby, twenty-one

My mom was nineteen years when she hooked up with a guy who got her pregnant. As soon as he received that news, he vanished. Consequently, I have never met my biological father.

My mother married another fellow named Harold when I was two or three years old. I suffered terrible verbal and emotional abuse from him. He would say stuff like I was worthless and would never amount to anything. On other occasions, I can remember asking for my mother to tuck me in at night, but my stepfather would throw ice-cold water on me and tell me to shut up. Perhaps that's why I was an angry young child when I started elementary school.

You know how the schoolyard can be—there are always kids picking fights. The first time I was ever confronted by another kid, I backed off. I came home and told Harold what happened.

"This guy wanted to fight me. Mom said don't

fight, so I walked away," I explained as only a seven-year-old could.

"If you ever walk away from a fight again, I'm gonna give you something to really cry about," he said, balling up his fists and striking the fear of God inside me. I never came home walking away from a fight again. I kept track: I was in fifty-two fights in grade school, winning fifty and losing two. One of my losses was to a guy named Antonio Wallace, a big black guy four years older than me. We were in the woods near our apartment complex. We started arguing, and the next thing I knew, he was pummeling me. I had a black and blue eye after that fight. My other loss was to Ricky Kitchens, a spiky-blond fellow. I hit the kid once, and that was the only time. He split my face open, but he was three or four years older than I was.

Like I said, those were my only losses. Most kids were pretty banged up after I got through with them. One time this kid named Tommy whacked me with his toy gun on the back of the head. Harold had to run me down to the emergency room for some stitches.

Tommy's mother tracked me down after I left the hospital because she knew of my reputation. "Don't beat my son up," she pleaded. "He didn't realize what he was doing. I apologize for him. Don't beat him up because he didn't mean to."

"All right. I won't do anything to him," I promised.

Two weeks later, Dad was driving me to school when we saw Tommy. Dad stopped the car. "Get out and beat him up," he ordered.

"Dad, I promised his mother that I wouldn't beat him up."

"You can take him."

"That's not the point. I'm not going to."

Then there was an awkward moment of silence between us. He really wanted me to get out and deck him.

I'm telling you, I had a different upbringing. I had a younger sister and an older sister, and we all had different fathers. Mom worked as a bookkeeper at our apartment complex, while my stepfather worked in a restaurant. Then the apartment complex brought in new management, and Mom was out of a job. Money was really scarce, but my stepfather had an idea: we could move into another apartment with two gay guys he knew at the restaurant.

There were only two bedrooms, and the two guys shared one, of course. I slept on a couch next to the guys' bedroom. I had known about the birds and the bees since I was five years old. Even in first and second grade I liked to take girls into the bushes and kiss them and lie on top of them, just like I had seen it done in movies. Of course, I was not sexually mature at that age, but I liked the close physical contact.

The gay guys had a homemade door that didn't close very well. I could see them naked in their bedroom, and I had to take my eyes away from what I saw.

Living with the gay couple was seen as a transition until we could get on our feet again. Harold suggested that my mom, my two sisters, and me go live with relatives in Connecticut, and then he would move up from Orlando as soon as we got settled.

The four of us squeezed into a Ford Escort for the long drive. All our belongings were in the small sedan. It wasn't much. I had a pillow and a few clothes. My only toy was some baseball cards.

We moved in with my aunt and uncle in a two-bedroom duplex. Oh, did I tell you that my grandma also lived there? Five of us shared one bedroom. I started school, and we all waited for Harold to show up.

He never left Orlando. It seems that he had met some waitress at the restaurant, and he moved in with her.

That's when the divorce proceedings started. Mom was up a creek. No money coming in. Bills following her. She went to work in a dental office with my aunt. As I look back, I can see that's when my emotions did a flip-flop. I went from being a strong, calm individual to a person who walked around downcast with a hunched back. Before I thought I could conquer the world. Now I couldn't conquer eating a meal.

We moved back to Orlando after three months because Mom had to see the divorce through. From eleven to fifteen years of age, I started getting into trouble, skipping school, and doing acts of vandalism. I hated my nomadic life. I haven't discussed all twenty-six places that we lived, or the fourteen different schools I attended, or the time I lived in a garage and slept on a sofa bed with my mom and my sisters. We were so poor at times that we couldn't afford to buy water.

Life just plain stunk for me.

I started being disrespectful to Mom. I started mutilating myself. I can remember running into a real brick wall and banging my head against it just to see what it would feel like. I cut myself with a knife, usually on the arms. I punched myself in the face—whap, whap, whap, and kept it going. One place we lived had a metal door, and I punched it out so often that they had to replace the metal doors twice because of the dings I banged into it with my bare fists.

I began to experiment sexually with animals when I was eleven years old. In addition, at that age I began to touch girls in their personal areas without their permission. I've had sex with girls more than 130 times, by my count.

By age fifteen, I was as out of control as you could be. I attended school one day a week, on average. That's when Mom enrolled me in House of Hope in December 1996.

I'm not proud of how I got there, but I'm proud that I was the first male resident of House of Hope. At the time, though, I wasn't very happy. I tried everything to get kicked out. I got in physical fights with the staff. I would go into the community kitchen, take food out of the pantry and fridge, and throw it around. I peed on the floor in the classroom, and I peed my name on the floor in the teachers' office. I looked for ways to shut off the electricity.

About a year into the program, on November 11, 1997, I was driving in a car one afternoon with Mary Trotter, the executive director. She had been trying to get through to me for so long. I looked at her and said, "If this Jesus you're talking about is real, and

He really does love me and He'll help me, then I want to know whether He is who you say He is. So you tell me whatever prayer it is that I have to pray. Let's get this thing on the road because I'm tired of doing things my way."

We were at a red light, and she said, "Well, Bob, I never thought I'd hear those words from your mouth."

I looked at her with this hard look.

"There's no stereotypical prayer," she said. "All you have to do is to tell Jesus that you're sorry for your sins, that you want to serve Him and love Him."

I did that in the car that afternoon, right at 4:11 p.m.

After I finished making that prayer, I said, "What do I do now?"

"Don't worry," she said.

The first thing God had me deal with was my anger. I started studying about anger in Proverbs and how I should treat other people. That was a big first step. Next, I began to understand that God is my father, not the guy named Harold who would hold me by the neck and strangle me when he got angry with me, or hit my sister with a screwdriver because she didn't have the right attitude.

Remember in the beginning when I told you that I had never met my biological father? I could never understand how a man could father a child and then just leave. I felt somewhat empty inside, not sure of who I was, where I came from, or why I acted or looked as I do. Father's Day was always a struggle for me. All I could think about was all the other kids who were spending the day having lunch with their dads or playing catch with their fathers while I was at home alone wondering who my dad was.

I discovered that God the Father could love me like a father. Romans 8:14 says those who are led by the Spirit of God are sons of God. Verse 22 in that same chapter says we "groan inwardly as we wait eagerly for our adoption as sons, the redemption of our bodies." What really sealed the deal for me was 2 Corinthians 2:18: "I will be a Father to you, and you will be my sons and daughters, says the Lord Almighty."

My spiritual roots began at House of Hope, and for that I am very thankful. If it were not for their love and obedience to Christ, I am afraid to think of where I would be today. These days, I'm working with a medical sales company by day while earning my bachelors' degree in business administration by night. I've been with the company for nearly four years, and last year, we did $51 billion in sales. It's great to be part of that. I am actively involved with a great church, and I have recently been exploring my musical talents.

My future is bright because I have a Father who can lead me. I'm trying to walk as close as I can in His footsteps. I challenge you to do the same. I choose to be led by the Spirit as the Scripture says in Romans 8:14-16. . . .

. . . . those who are led by the Spirit of God are sons of God. For you did not receive a spirit that makes you a slave again to fear, but you received the Spirit of sonship. And by him we cry, "Abba, Father." The Spirit himself testifies with our spirit that we are God's children.

—Romans 8:14-16, NIV

a final thought

from sheila walsh

national spokesperson for House of Hope

At House of Hope, we have a life message. It's a very simple one—God loves you! God loves *you* right now no matter what's going on in your life.

Sometimes it's easy to believe that if there is a God, He might love people who make good choices, go to church on Sunday morning, and follow all the rules. But what about those of us who mess up time after time? Could God love even us? The answer is yes, yes, yes!

A friend of mine once asked me to imagine that a movie had been made of my life and nothing had been left out. Everything I had ever done or thought about doing was up there on the screen for anyone who wanted to watch it. She asked me how I would feel about that. I told her that I'd be on the first plane out of here! Then she reminded me of a life-changing truth. "Sheila," she said, "God has seen your movie, and He loves you."

Do you understand that? Can you grab hold of that for your own life? God knows everything you have ever said or done, and He is still crazy about you!

In *Unglued, Tattooed & Renewed,* you've read the stories of those whose lives were changed forever by the love of God. Many of these teenagers first heard the Good News through Sara Trollinger and the staff at House of Hope. Many people talk about the love of God, but Sara and her staff live it out every single day.

As you look at your own life, you might wonder the following two questions:

- Where was God when terrible things were happening to me?
- If God is so good, why is life so hard sometimes?

Those are great questions, and I don't have answers big enough to fill the places that have been carved out in your soul. But I can tell you that I have seen with my own eyes what God can do when you come to Him just as you are and say, "God I don't know a lot about you, but I want to. I want to know your love. I want a new heart and a new beginning. I'm sorry for the ways I've messed up. Can we start again? Thank you!"

God says you can start again, no matter what, because:

"For God so loved the world that he gave his one and only Son, that whoever believes in him shall not perish but have eternal life" (John 3:16, NIV).

Everyone longs to find a place where everything about us is known and where we are loved and accepted. There is such a place—the arms of the Father God who made you and who loves you.

Let me close with the words of a simple song written in 1860, but the words are true for you today:

Jesus loves me! This I know,
For the Bible tells me so.
Little ones to Him belong;
They are weak, but He is strong.

Yes, Jesus loves me!
Yes, Jesus loves me!
Yes, Jesus loves me!
The Bible tells me so.

Jesus loves me! This I know,
As He loved so long ago,
Taking children on His knee,
Saying, "Let them come to Me."

Yes, Jesus loves me!
Yes, Jesus loves me!
Yes, Jesus loves me!
The Bible tells me so.

Jesus loves me! He who died
Heaven's gate to open wide;
He will wash away my sin,
Let His little child come in.

Yes, Jesus loves me!
Yes, Jesus loves me!
Yes, Jesus loves me!
The Bible tells me so.

Would You Like to Learn More About Starting a House of Hope?

House of Hope's idea is spreading nationally! Homes for troubled teens, based on the successful counseling and educational program of the model House of Hope in Orlando, Florida, are opening around the country. If you would like to learn more about House of Hope or attend a training seminar, please contact:

Sara Trollinger
House of Hope
P.O. Box 560503
Orlando, FL 32856
(407) 843-8686
e-mail: houseofhopesara@aol.com
Web site: www.nationalhouseofhope.org

If you would like to request copies of Sara Trollinger's first book, *Unglued & Tattooed: How to Save Your Teen from Raves, Ritalin, Goth, Body Carving, GHB, Sex, and 12 Other Emerging Threats*, contact House of Hope at the above address or phone number. Hardback copies are available for a suggested donation of $19.95. All proceeds go toward starting Houses of Hope across America.